Microsoft® PowerPoint® 2000 MOUS

by Doug Klippert

A Division of Macmillan USA
201 W. 103rd Street, Indianapolis, Indiana 46290

Microsoft® PowerPoint® 2000 MOUS Cheat Sheet

Copyright © 2000 by Que® Corporation

International Standard Book Number: 0-7897-2118-x

Library of Congress Catalog Card Number: 99-63522

Printed in the United States of America

First Printing: November 1999

01   00   99   4   3   2   1

Trademarks

Warning and Disclaimer

Associate Publisher *Jim Minatel*

Executive Editor *Angela Wethington*

Acquisitions Editor *Tracy Williams*

Series Editor *Jill Hayden*

Development Editor *Jill Hayden*

Managing Editor *Lisa Wilson*

Project Editor *Tonya Simpson*

Copy Editors *JoAnna Kremer, Pamela Woolf*

Indexer *Sharon Shock*

Proofreader *Megan Wade*

Technical Editor *Connie Myers*

Team Coordinator *Vicki Harding*

Media Developer *Andrea Duvall*

Interior Design *Barb Kordesh*

Cover Design *Tim Amrhein*

Copy Writer *Eric Borgert*

Production *Stacey DeRome, Heather Miller, Ayanna Lacey*

Dedication

To my friends and family who accepted the "I've got a deadline" excuse.

Acknowledgments

I would like to sincerely thank the people who put this book together. Jill Hayden and Tracy Williams juggled email and air mail to keep the whole thing on track. Connie Myers and Stephen J. Land kept the project from slipping away from the essentials. I would also like to recognize the hundreds of people who populate the Internet forums. There's a sense of us all being in this together. Truly, the help you give one person today will come back tenfold in the future.

Tell Us What You Think!

As the reader of this book, *you* are our most important critic and commentator. We value your opinion and want to know what we're doing right, what we could do better, what areas you'd like to see us publish in, and any other words of wisdom you're willing to pass our way.

As an Associate Publisher for Que, I welcome your comments. You can fax, email, or write me directly to let me know what you did or didn't like about this book—as well as what we can do to make our books stronger.

Please note that I cannot help you with technical problems related to the topic of this book, and that due to the high volume of mail I receive, I might not be able to reply to every message.

When you write, please be sure to include this book's title and author as well as your name and phone or fax number. I will carefully review your comments and share them with the author and editors who worked on the book.

Fax: 317-581-4666

Email: office_que@mcp.com

Mail: Associate Publisher
         Que Corporation
         201 West 103rd Street
         Indianapolis, IN 46290 USA

Introduction

There is only one level of competency that is tested for PowerPoint 2000. There, are, however, 51 skills that you are required to know to pass the exam.

Some of the activities that are covered by the PowerPoint 2000 exam are common to other programs, such as Excel or Word. You need to know how to run the Spell Checker, for instance. You might also be called upon to locate and replace text. By reading the chapters and completing the practice exercises in this book, you can make sure that you understand these basic skills. Knowing how to perform basic skills quickly might give you extra time to use with more time-consuming procedures.

There are only a few new features in PowerPoint 2000. If you are familiar with previous versions, this exam should not present any major difficulty. Make sure you understand each of the activities in the Objectives list—better to be over prepared than over confident.

How This Book Is Different

Unlike most PowerPoint books on the market, this book is strictly exam-focused. You will find that there are no tasks on the test that require you to use Visual Basic for Applications. Therefore, VBA is also not covered in this book.

Examine the Cheat Sheet to see if there are any skills that you have not used before, or that you have used only infrequently. Go through the Practice Lab until you can quickly do what's asked of you without relying on the book or the Help file; you will have little time to look up information during the test.

The tearcard that is included with this book outlines all the objectives. Here you will find alternative ways to perform the tasks; the only activities that are covered in this book are those that are required to pass the MOUS exam. You won't have to wade through material that, although it is good to know, is unrelated to the certification test.

How to Use This Book

Each chapter in this book covers a number of related activities, such as operations that focus on text. There is an Objectives Index in the back of the book that lists the official Objectives determined by the test distributor and the page number in this book where you will find the discussion of each objective.

At the end of each chapter there is a Cheat Sheet with a list of different ways to perform the action. Use this Cheat Sheet to review each chapter, both as you are progressing through the book and as a recap in the last few hours before the exam.

There is also a Practice Lab at the end of each chapter, in which you can practice the objectives you have learned. The tasks are in the same form as the real exam. To begin each practice lab, download the designated practice file from the CD-ROM. Then complete the tasks that are listed. When you have finished the last task of the practice lab, download and open the designated solution file to check your work. You'll know immediately if you need to review the objectives in that chapter.

You can remove the tearsheet that is included just inside the front cover of the book and use it to quiz yourself on the methods used. You can also take this card with you to the testing center for one last look before you enter the testing room.

The appendixes contain some thoughts about Exam Preparation. This exam is a little different than others you might have taken in that it is a hands-on test of your application savvy. Read what others have learned about successfully passing the tests.

What's New in Office 2000

Office 2000 has some characteristics that differ from previous versions. You need to be familiar with them so that you are not thrown for a loss when under pressure.

Personalized Menus

The menus and toolbars in Office 2000 show the most recently used items. They, in effect, customize themselves as you work. When PowerPoint is first opened you see only the basic menu items and buttons. As you continue to work with the program, the commands you use most often will start to appear, and others will go away.

The items that are shown on the short version of the built-in menu change with your use.

This can be disconcerting. At the bottom of the short version of the built-in menu there is an arrow that expands the menu to show all the commands. You can also double-click the menu or wait a few seconds for it to expand. Toolbars also have an arrow at the far right that displays more buttons.

Document Icons on the Taskbar

There is a change that shouldn't cause much of a problem in the examination. If you open two files at the same time, you can see two separate icons on the taskbar. To see both files at the same time, click the Window menu and select Arrange All. The Tile Windows command that appears when you right-click on the taskbar does not arrange the two files. This command only works with windows from separate programs, such as an instance of Word and an instance of PowerPoint.

Toolbar Addition

There is another button on the Formatting toolbar for Common Tasks, such as New Slide, Slide Layout, and Apply Design Template.

Contents

Chapter 8   Customizing a Presentation   99

Chapter 11   Managing Files   **133**

Creating a Presentation

PowerPoint gives you the tools you need to put together a presentation in several ways. There are many content and design templates that help coordinate the look of a show. You can start with an existing file and change it, or you can begin with a blank presentation and produce your own unique production. Whichever method is most appropriate, you will have the opportunity to customize the show to reflect your own needs and sense of style.

This skill set covers five objectives that relate to producing a presentation:

- Navigate Among Different Views (Slide, Outline, Sorter, Tri-Pane)
- Create a Presentation Using the AutoContent Wizard
- Create a Presentation from a Template or a Wizard
- Create a New Presentation from Existing Slides
- Create a Blank Presentation

1

Navigate Among Different Views (Slide, Outline, Sorter, Tri-Pane)

There are five views, or ways to look at the pieces that make up a slide show. This objective tests your capability to move from one of these views to another.

Open PowerPoint

A startup dialog box appears by default when PowerPoint is opened. The upper half of the box presents the options of creating a new presentation using an <u>A</u>utoContent Wizard or a Design <u>T</u>emplate, or opening a <u>B</u>lank presentation. The lower half of the box can be used to <u>O</u>pen an existing presentation.

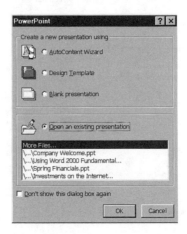

If the Startup dialog box is not displayed, each of these options can be found on the File menu. Click the File menu and select New to display the templates, or press Ctrl+N. To locate an existing file, click the File menu and select Open, or press Ctrl+O.

By default, PowerPoint 2000 opens a file with a Normal or *tri-pane* view. The tri-pane view gives you the opportunity to see the Outline View, the Slide View, and part of the Notes View at the same time. The other major view option is Slide Sorter View. These two views can be used to do almost all the work needed to put a presentation together.

To navigate between views, use either the View menu or the Views bar at the bottom-left corner of the screen.

Click the Zoom box on the Standard toolbar, or click the View menu and select Zoom to change the magnification of the text or slide of the selected pane. Following are the descriptions of the five views.

Normal View is the default opening view. If you are in another view, click ▣ Normal View on the Views bar, or click the View menu and select Normal. The Normal view displays the Outline, Slide, and Note panes.

You will probably do a great deal of your work in this view. The only real difference between Normal and Outline View is the amount of space allotted for each pane. The panes can be resized by positioning the pointer over the dividers between the panes and dragging with the left mouse button. As the Slide pane changes dimension, the size of the slide changes proportionately.

On the left side of the view is the Outline pane. The upper-right corner displays a view of the slide, and the lower-right provides a space to add notes. The user can edit in any one of the panes.

Be aware of the difference between Outline View and the Outline Pane. Outline View is a display of different objects in the show, and the Outline Pane is the portion of the window that shows an outline of the presentation.

The Note Page View icon from PowerPoint 97 is gone and is replaced by the Normal View icon.

Normal View

Outline Pane

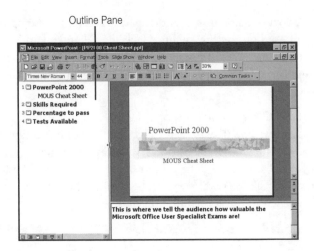

Outline View

Click ▤ Outline View on the Views bar to display the outline of your show with the text and a miniature of the slide. Outline View is not accessible through the View menu. All discussion about the Outline view also holds true for Normal View. You also have access to the Notes pane, as you do in Normal view. Text can be edited here, and you also have the opportunity to change the order or number of slides in the show.

The Outline pane is the quickest way to add text to slides and to promote or demote heading levels. When text is added to the outline, the title and body text of the slides are also placed in text placeholders on the slides.

The ▥ Expand All button on the Formatting toolbar collapses or expands the lower-level text so that only the slide title is seen, or so that all text can be viewed and edited.

The best way to navigate between slides when you are in either Normal or Outline view depends on which pane has focus. If your insertion point is in the Outline pane, you can move from slide to slide by pressing the arrow keys on the keyboard, or by just clicking into the text of the slide. The vertical scrollbar only shows more text—it does not change to another slide. If the Slide itself is selected, you can press the Page Up or Page Down keys to navigate. The scrollbar to the right of the slide also displays the next slide. Use the scrollbar slider to see a screen tip that shows the slide number and title.

The scrollbar on the Notes pane only shows you more of the text contained in the Note.

Click ▣ Slide View on the View bar to show a full view of a single slide. The Slide View button does not appear on the View menu. You can use Slide View to edit the text or graphics or to change the formatting of just one slide in the series (as discussed in Objectives 14, "Change the Layout for One or More Slides," and 17, "Change and Replace Text Fonts (Individual Slide and Entire Presentation)). This view enables you to see just the slide, without the distraction of the Outline or Notes pane.

Slide View

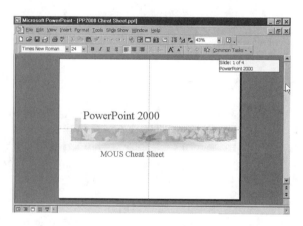

Press the Page Up or Page Down keys to change slides. The scrollbar to the right of the slide can also be used to navigate, and it displays the name of the slide.

Click ▦ Slide Sorter View, or click the View menu and select Slide Sorter, to display all your slides as preview miniatures. You can change the order of the show, the timing, and the slide transitions here. Slides can be deleted or copied in this view.

Slide Sorter View

This is a good view to see the overall graphical construction of the presentation. Notes and Outline panes are absent. The Drawing toolbar is not displayed in Slide Sorter View.

You cannot edit individual slides in this view, but if you double-click on a slide, PowerPoint switches to Slide View.

Press keyboard arrow keys to move the focus from slide to slide.

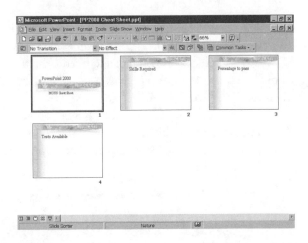

Slide Show View

Click Slide Show View on the Views bar, or click Views and select Slide Show, to run the show and display the slides full-size on the screen. This is also a way to quickly review how each slide will appear. You can stop the show by pressing the Esc key. (A fast way to start a slide show is to just press the F5 key.)

To change slides, click the mouse or press the Enter key. Press the Page Up and Page Down keys to navigate during the slide show. For information on automated slide transitions, see Objective 35 in Chapter 8, "Customizing a Presentation."

The Notes Page includes a miniature view of the slide and a place to write notes. These can be notes to yourself about the show, used as speaker's notes or as part of the handout material. To look at a full-screen view of the Notes page, click the View menu and select Notes Page. To navigate, drag the scrollbar or press the Page Up and Page Down keys to show the next or previous notes.

Notes Page

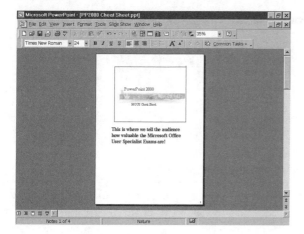

Create a Presentation Using the AutoContent Wizard

PowerPoint includes a wizard to assist you in putting a show together. The AutoContent Wizard helps you determine the type of slide show you need, its style, and some common elements used in various presentations.

Start the Wizard

The AutoContent Wizard can be started from the opening dialog box (refer to the first figure of this chapter). Or, to start the Wizard from within PowerPoint, click the File menu and select New. On the General tab of the New Presentation dialog box, choose the AutoContent Wizard icon to open the AutoContent Wizard Start screen.

The Office Assistant offers help if you click the question mark button in the lower-left corner.

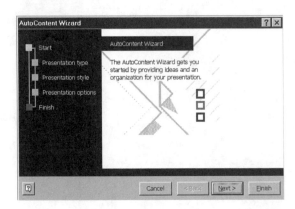

From the AutoContent Wizard Start screen, click Next to advance to the Presentation Type screen. The various templates are grouped by category.

Select the category of show you want to use, and then click Next to continue.

You can change your mind later, but it's good practice to begin with an idea about how your show will be presented.

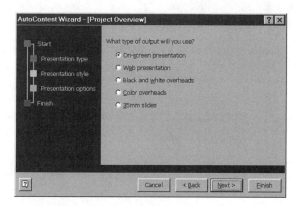

The dimensions of the slides and how colors are used vary depending on how your show is to be delivered. The show can be reformatted later, but you will probably have to correct the layout if the dimensions change. In the Presentation Style dialog box, select the output for your presentation and click Next to continue.

The fourth screen, Presentation Options, has an area to insert a title for the presentation and text for the footer, such as the company name. You can edit all this later if necessary.

You do not need to enter anything in these boxes. The Date and Slide number are selected by default. You might be asked to deselect Date last updated and Slide number if they're not needed in the show.

When you click the Next button this time, you are given one more opportunity to go Back and change your entries or the type of presentation. This is your last chance. When the Finish button is clicked, PowerPoint opens your presentation in Normal View, ready for you to work on the new show. To go back to the wizard, you must go back to the File menu and select New to start fresh.

View the Results

Depending on the style of presentation you have chosen, the text in the Outline pane will suggest points that need to be covered. You don't need to use all the suggested content and, of course, you can add more text or slides. However, if you follow these suggested guidelines, you won't go far wrong.

At this point, you can edit and change the slides to fit your requirements. PowerPoint has just given you a skeleton to flesh out.

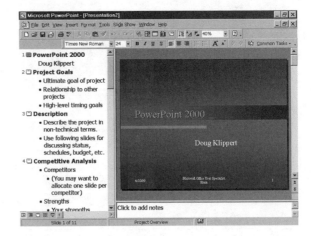

Create a Presentation from a Template or a Wizard

You can roll your own show, starting with a template. Go to the File menu and select New, or press Ctrl+N. To create a new presentation, you can choose a template from one of the tabs on the New Presentation dialog box.

The General tab is used for a Blank Presentation Template and the AutoContent Wizard. Blank Presentations are covered in Objective 5, "Create a Blank Presentation."

The Design Templates tab has templates that have been put together with graphics, fonts, and colors that are complementary. These templates enable you to put together a pleasing show with little effort.

Design Templates

Lorem ipsum dolor sit amet is nonsense text used to demonstrate text layout.

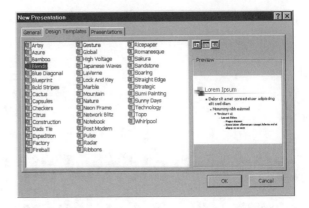

Unlike the templates used by the AutoContent Wizard, Design templates produce slides with just the color and layout design—without suggested text. There are two masters in each template: a Title Master and a regular Slide Master.

Applying a Design Template will be covered in Objective 9, "Apply a Design Template."

Presentations The Presentations tab on the New Presentation box holds the same templates that are used by the AutoContent Wizard. You won't be held by the hand when you select a topic, and although you might be called upon to use the AutoContent Wizard for the examination, I think you'll find it just as easy to open one of these templates directly and then customize the text. Presentation templates include several slides and suggested topic items to assist in putting a show together.

Presentations template slides do have placeholders for suggested text.

Placeholders ———

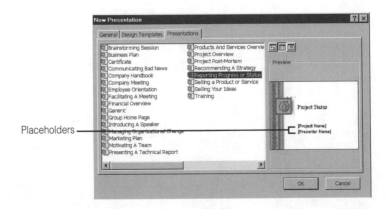

Create a New Presentation from Existing Slides

After you've put together a successful presentation, it can be useful to use that show as the backbone of a new presentation. To clone an existing show, open and rename it.

If you have just started PowerPoint and the startup dialog box is open, you can select Open an existing presentation. If the file is not in the most recently opened files list, select More Files and click OK to open the file to be copied.

Open a Show

The original show can also be found by clicking the File menu and selecting Open, or by pressing Ctrl+O.

When the show opens, go back to the File menu and choose Save As, or press the F12 key. Verify the location in the Save in box and then give the file a new name. You now have a copy of the original show and can make any changes needed for the new presentation.

Save a Copy

This technique is most useful if there are a good number of slides and reusable text from the old show. If some of the slides are not needed, they can be deleted. The rest can be edited or reordered to make a new presentation. You can also copy slides from one show to another, which is covered in Objective 6, "Copy a Slide from One Presentation into Another."

5

Create a Blank Presentation

PowerPoint opens with a selection dialog box. The third option button opens a blank presentation. If PowerPoint is already open, you have three options to start a blank presentation:

- Click ☐ New on the Standard toolbar.
- Click the File menu and select New.
- Press Ctrl+N on the keyboard.

On the General tab, choose the template for a Blank presentation.

Which Slide to Use

When you create a blank presentation, the first choice you have to make is what format of AutoLayout slide you want to use. Choosing Blank Presentation opens the New Slide dialog box.

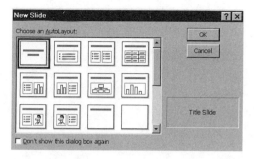

The blank presentation has no design styles applied to it, except for the plain vanilla default master.

The dialog box presents 24 AutoLayouts. The preset layouts have objects already included for most of the common setups such as Text&Clip Art, Chart&Text, Two-Column Text, and others. There is also a layout for an empty blank slide.

There are placeholders for objects, depending on the layout that was picked, but the content and design are entirely up to you. The placeholders make it easy to set up organizational charts or insert pictures. The layouts with graphs, for example, include a placeholder that starts an applet to create original charts when an icon is double-clicked.

For information on how to apply design templates to an existing show, see Objective 9; to learn how to reformat and edit text, see Objectives 15–19.

TAKE THE TEST

Task 1

This task covers Objective 1, "Navigate Among Different Views," and Objective 2, "Create a Presentation Using the AutoContent Wizard." To begin this task, start PowerPoint 2000.

The exam will assume that you can interpret the instructions. For example, in the first directions you are asked to report on the progress of a project. You will be expected to locate the appropriate template using the AutoContent Wizard. There are no tricks. The actual questions won't be any more difficult than the ones that follow:

1. Create a presentation, using the AutoContent Wizard, that will report on the progress of a project. The show will be delivered onscreen. Name the presentation New Sales Status. Do not include the date updated or the slide number in this show. The footer should say General Sales Company.

2. Switch to Slide Sorter View.

3. Save the file as Sales Status in the PP2000 folder.

The solution file for this task is Ch01-Sales Status.ppt.

To check your work, open Ch01-Sales Status.ppt. Then open your answer, C:\PP2000\Sales Status.ppt. Click Window on the Menu bar and choose Arrange All. The two shows will be displayed side by side.

This task covers Objective 3, "Create a Presentation from a Template or a Wizard."

1. Create a new show based on the Brainstorming session template. Enter the title of the first slide as Creativity Session.

2. Enter the presenter's name as Lisa Fox.

3. Save the file as Brainstorm in the PP2000 folder.

To check your work, open Ch01-Brainstorm.ppt. Then open your answer, C:\PP2000\Brainstorm.ppt. Click Window on the Menu bar and choose Arrange All. The two shows will be displayed side by side.

This task covers Objective 4, "Create a New Presentation from Existing Slides."

(This same skill will be tested in the next chapter, when deleting slides is introduced.)

1. Create a new show named Annual Brainstorm from the file Brainstorm.PPT in the Practice Lab.

2. Save the new file in the PP2000 folder.

The solution file for this task is Ch01-Annual Brainstorm.ppt. To check your work, open Ch01-Annual Brainstorm.ppt. Then open your answer, C:\PP2000\Annual Brainstorm.ppt. Click Window on the Menu bar and choose Arrange All. The two shows will be displayed side by side.

This task covers Objective 5, "Create a Blank Presentation."

1. Create a blank presentation with just a Title Only slide.

2. Enter Basic Presentation as the slide title.

3. Save the file as Basic Presentation in the PP2000 folder.

The solution file for this task is Ch01-Basic Presentation.ppt. To check your work, open Ch01- Basic Presentation.ppt. Then open your answer, C:\PP2000\ Basic Presentation.ppt. Click Window on the Menu bar and choose Arrange All. The two shows will be displayed side by side. There are directions for the task in Objective 5.

Cheat Sheet

View and Edit Tri-Pane

▣	Normal View	(View, Normal)
▤	Outline View	No menu item
▥	Slide View	No menu item

Rearrange Order or Delete Slides

▦	Slide Sorter	(View, Slide Sorter)

View the Show

▣	Slide Show	(View, Slide Show)	or press F5

View or Edit Speaker Notes and Slide

(No Icon)	Notes Page	(View, Notes Page)

AutoContent Wizard

1. File, New, General tab, AutoContent Wizard.
2. Date last updated and Slide number can be deselected.

Design Templates (Just Color and Layout Design; No Sample Text)

File, New, Design Templates tab.

Presentation Templates (Color, Layout Design, and Sample Text)

File, New, Presentation Templates.

Create a New Presentation from Existing Slides

1. File, Save As (or F12).
2. Give the existing file a new name.

Cheat Sheet

Create a Blank Presentation

1. File, <u>N</u>ew, General Tab, Blank Presentation template.

2. Choose a layout, probably the Title slide.

Tools for Creating a Presentation

You don't need to start over every time you produce a prsentation. You can work with pieces created for other shows, or elements can be imported from other applications and slide shows.

Following are four more skills used to construct a PowerPoint show:

- Copy a Slide from One Presentation into Another
- Create a Specified Type of Slide
- Delete Slides
- Apply a Design Template

These tasks deal with the placement of the slides themselves. Editing individual slides is covered in later chapters.

Copy a Slide from One Presentation into Another

That great slide you put together for the sales rollout is just right for the boss's birthday show. Here's how to use slides from other presentations.

Copy and Paste

Open the presentation that contains the slides you want to duplicate. Change to Slide Sorter view. Select as many slides as you want using the Ctrl key. Copy the slides by using one of the following methods:

- Click the Edit menu or right-click to open the shortcut menu and select Copy.

- Press Ctrl+C.

- Press 📋 Copy on the Standard toolbar.

Open the target file and place the insertion point where you want to place the copied slides. Paste the slides by using one of the following methods:

- Click the Edit menu or right-click to open the shortcut menu and select Paste.

- Press Ctrl+V.

- Press 📋 Paste on the Standard toolbar.

To use Insert, select the slide that precedes the slide you want to insert. Click the Insert menu and select Slides from Files. The Slide Finder dialog box gives you the chance to Browse and locate the file.

The Look In drop-down list contains all the drives and folders attached to your machine. If the folder you need is not displayed, click 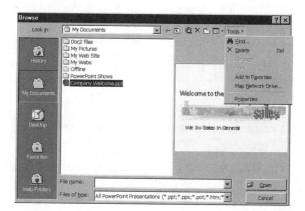 Up One Level. Another way is to click on the root of the drive (C:\), and then drill down until you find the right directory.

It is not guaranteed that all the files used in the test will be located in the same folder. Get accustomed to maneuvering up and down the directory tree.

If you must search further, click Tools on the top right side of the Browse dialog box and select Find.

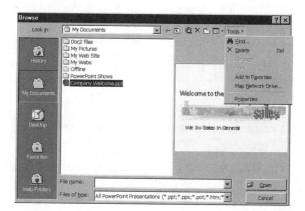

When you locate the correct file, double-click to open it.

Scroll until you locate the slide that's being called for. If you are just given the title of the slide, click the left button of the two that are located in the middle of the Slide Finder box. This displays all the titles in the left box and a preview on the right.

If you want to insert more than one slide, hold down the Ctrl key while selecting slides and choose Insert. To copy an entire presentation, click Insert All.

You can insert copies of all the files, or you can select individual slides to add to your new presentation.

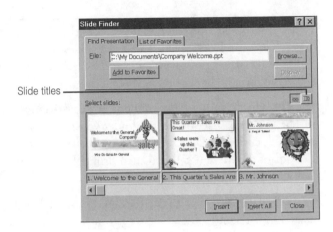

Slide titles

Drag and Drop

Another method for moving slides from one presentation to another is to open both presentations in Slide Sorter view. You can drag slides from one presentation to another. To copy the slide rather than move it, hold down the Ctrl key and drag. To have better control over moving or copying slides, use the right mouse button. The shortcut menu provides alternatives.

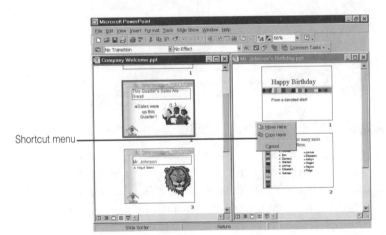

Shortcut menu

There's a small change with Office 2000: When you have two documents or slide shows open, you might see a separate icon for each file on the taskbar. Avoid the temptation to use the old trick of right-clicking on the taskbar to arrange windows—this does not work! Go to Window, Arrange All in PowerPoint to tile the windows.

Create a Specified Type of Slide

The slide layouts are used to quickly position elements on a slide. Some of the layouts include icons that start up an applet such as Microsoft Clip Gallery.

When a new presentation is opened, PowerPoint displays a New Slide dialog box with two dozen predesigned slide layouts. An AutoLayout template is a slide with placeholders for text, graphics, charts, or other types of objects. In addition to a pre-view of the slide, a description of the slide is displayed.

AutoLayout

There are three methods for inserting a new slide:

- Click the Insert menu and select New slide.

- Press Ctrl+M.

- The Formatting toolbar has an area called Common Tasks. If you click this button, you can choose New Slide.

It's wise to know several alternative ways to do the same job.

The new slide is inserted after the insertion point in Slide Layout view or Outline View. In Outline view, the new slide will come before the existing slide if the insertion point is at the beginning of the slide text.

New Slides Follow

Delete Slides

Not every slide is a keeper, and not every slide is needed. Deleting slides is an ongoing exercise. There are a couple of ways to do it.

Use the Keyboard

Click the Edit menu and choose Delete Slide in any editing view. While you are in Slide Layout view, you can select a slide and press the Delete key on the keyboard.

Be warned that with the new menu system that is used by Office 2000, you probably have to wait the three or four seconds, or click on the expansion chevrons, to make the Delete Slide entry appear.

Pick a Bunch

To delete more than one slide at a time, hold down the Ctrl key while selecting slides in Slide Sorter view. If the slides are together, you can use the Shift key to select contiguous slides.

Slides can also be deleted from the Outline pane. In the Outline pane, the Shift key works to group slides, but the Ctrl key does not.

Put Them on the Clipboard

Slides can be removed from the presentation using the Cut command:

- Click the Edit menu and select Cut.
- Press [✄] Cut on the Standard toolbar or on the shortcut menu that appears after you right-click the mouse.
- Press Ctrl+X.

Remember that cut slides are now stored on the Clipboard. Because the Office Clipboard stores more than just one entry, you can probably use this to cut and paste more than one slide. The Office Clipboard is covered in Objective 24, "Use the Office Clipboard."

Apply a Design Template

Design templates provide a preset collection of color schemes, font styles, and graphic objects. Sometimes you might want to change the design used on an existing show. Also, some colors and backgrounds show up better, depending on lighting or projection conditions.

To change the existing design template, just click the Format menu and select Apply Design Template. The dialog box lists the existing designs and shows a preview. Choose one and click Apply. The design is applied to every slide in the show.

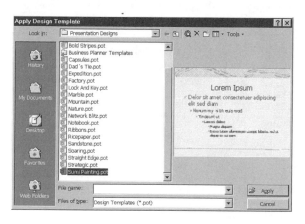

Use the arrow keys on the keyboard to move up and down the list.

You might have to make adjustments because the design template might use a different typeface or point size. The placeholders also might be in a different location because of the graphics used in the design.

TAKE THE TEST

Task 1

This task covers Objective 4, "Create a New Presentation from Existing Slides," and Objective 8, "Delete Slides."

1. Open General Brainstorm from the Practice Lab.

2. Delete slides 7, 8, and 9.

3. Save the file as C:\PP2000\Short General.ppt.

The solution file for this task is Ch02- Short General.ppt. To check your work, open Ch02- Short General.ppt. Then open your answer, C:\PP2000\Short General.ppt. Click Window on the Menu bar and choose Arrange All. The two shows will be displayed side by side.

Task 2

This task covers Objective 6, "Copy a Slide from One Presentation into Another"; Objective 7, "Create a Specified Type of Slide"; and Objective 9, "Apply a Design Template." To begin this task, open the Short.ppt file from the CD.

The exam can and will cover more than one objective in each question. There are 51 objectives, but there will be fewer than 51 questions.

1. Change the design format to Nature.

2. Place Slide 1 from the Practice Lab: General Sales Company.ppt as the first slide of Short.PPT.

3. Add a blank Title slide as the last slide.

4. Save the file as c:\PP2000\The General's Short.PPT.

The solution file for this task is Ch02- The General's Short.ppt. To check your work, open Ch02- The General's Short.ppt. Then open your answer, C:\PP2000\The General's Short.ppt. Click Window on the Menu bar and choose Arrange All. The two shows will be displayed side by side.

Cheat Sheet

Copy a Slide from One Presentation into Another

1. Insert, Slides from Files.

2. Browse to locate second file.

3. Display slides.

4. Select a slide and click Insert.

Or

1. Open both shows.

2. Window, Arrange All.

3. Hold down Ctrl and drag slides from one show to another.

Create a Specified Type of Slide

Insert, New Slide, select the correct layout, and click OK.

Delete Slides

Select a slide and press Delete, or use Edit, Delete Slide.

Apply a Design Template

Format, Apply Design Template, select a design, click Apply.

Modifying a Presentation

You have a great deal of design freedom in producing a PowerPoint show. This skill set covers how to edit a PowerPoint show, as well as some of the ways the presentation can be rearranged. The following areas are covered:

- Change the Order of Slides Using Slide Sorter View
- Modify Slide Sequence in the Outline Pane
- Change Slide Layout (Modify the Slide Master)
- Insert Headers and Footers
- Change the Layout for One or More Slides

10

Change the Order of Slides Using Slide Sorter View

The Slide Sorter view gives you a fast look at how your show is sequenced. You can change the order of slides as if they were laid out on a tabletop. To get to Slide Sorter View, click ▦ Slide Sorter View on the Views bar, or click View and select Slide Sorter.

Drag and Drop

The pointer also carries a box on its tail when you are moving a slide.

As you hold down the left mouse button and drag the slide, a gray vertical line indicates where the slide is to be dropped.

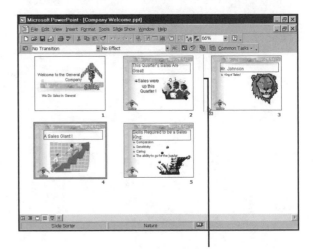

Slide location

Right-click the mouse as you drag a slide to display a shortcut menu with the choices of Move Here, Copy Here, or Cancel.

If you want to select several slides at the same time, use the Ctrl key while choosing slides. If you need to select a series of slides, the Shift key selects all the slides from the first selection to the last.

Choose More than One

You can also hold down the left mouse button and drag across the slides. First click *in front* of the slides you want to select, and then drag. Be warned, though: If you have a slide selected, you will move it rather than include it in the copy group.

Be careful with the Ctrl key. Release the key before moving the slides. If you hold down the Ctrl key when the mouse button is released, you will create copies of the original slides rather than just move them.

11

Modify Slide Sequence in the Outline Pane

The Outline pane shows the text on each slide and presents an ordered list of the slides. The pointer turns into a four-headed arrow when it hovers over the slide icon next to the number of the slide.

By holding down the left mouse button, you can move the slide up or down the list.

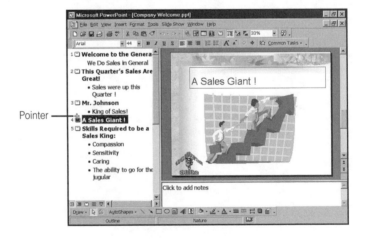

Holding down the Shift key enables you to select a scries of slides to move. The Ctrl key does not work in the Outline pane. Right-clicking the mouse enables you to cut, copy, or paste, but it does not show the Move/Copy menu.

The Outline view enables you to move text from one slide to another. To make sure that you are moving the whole slide, and not just a subtitle or body text, click to turn off ▥ Expand All on the Standard toolbar. Expand All also toggles on and off with Alt+Shift+9.

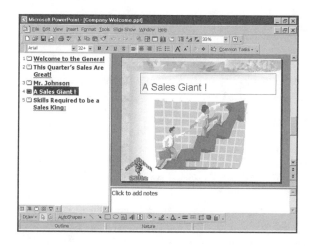

When Expand All is toggled off, only the title of the slide shows.

12

Change Slide Layout (Modify the Slide Master)

A presentation will hold the audience's attention better if it has a feeling of continuity. To help you create slides that have common elements, PowerPoint uses a kind of template called a master. There are master models for regular slides, the title slide, handouts, and notes.

Open the Master

To change the layout of the normal slide, open the View menu, point to Master, and choose Slide Master. You can also open the Master by holding down the Shift key when you click [⊡] Slide View on the Views bar. Three layout areas can be customized on this template: the title of the slide, the body, and the footer area. Change the formatting of the placeholder text to format all slides except the title slide.

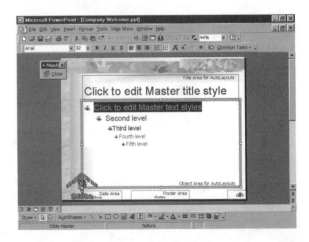

You can change the font type, size, and color on the master: Select the text that is included in a placeholder and use the Formatting toolbar, or click the Format menu and select Font to open the Font dialog box.

Change the Typeface

The placeholder area itself can also be formatted. Click the Format menu and select Placeholder, or right-click the mouse to open the shortcut menu, and then pick Format Placeholder to open the Format AutoShape dialog box.

If just the text in a placeholder is formatted, that particular piece of text keeps the formatting. If you format a text box or placeholder, any new entries will have the default formatting.

To go back to the default settings, click Format, Apply Design Template. Reapply the original design. Any text or graphics that were added are not replaced, and the fonts and color schemes are reset.

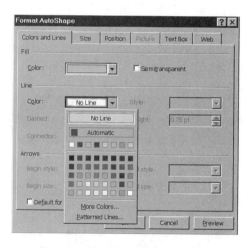

Changes that are made to the Slide Master are reflected on all the slides in the show. You can put a company logo or your name on each slide by editing the Slide Master and inserting the logo as a picture.

Universal Changes

13

Insert Headers and Footers

As with a regular document, you might want information to appear on every slide. For example, you might want the title of the show, the name of the company, the date, or the slide number to be displayed on every slide. Headers and footers are associated with the Slide Master, but you can insert or edit them without opening the master templates.

View Header/ Footer

To work on headers or footers, click the View menu, point to View, and select Header and Footer to open the Header and Footer dialog box.

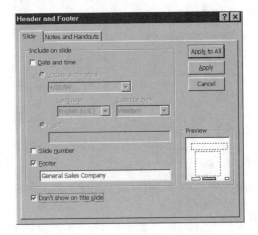

The dialog box's Slide tab gives you the opportunity to apply the date, slide number, or text to the footer of a slide. You can apply the text to all slides, or you can exclude the title slide by checking Don't Show on Title Slide. The preview box in the lower-right corner shows the placeholders for each item. If the text boxes are changed on the Master, the Preview box shows the change.

The data can also be restricted to just one slide. If you click the Apply button, the selected slide alone displays the information. Apply to All changes every slide in the presentation.

Change Only One Slide

The Notes and Handouts tab has input areas for the headers and footers of notes and handouts. Notes and handouts are formatted as a group. You can format single notes in the Notes Pane or in Notes Page view.

14

Change the Layout for One or More Slides

The layout of a slide is usually chosen when a new slide is inserted, but there might come a time when you want to change it. For example, you might want to switch the text and picture positions on a slide to add variety, you might want a different background on some slides, or you might want to suppress the header and footer for design reasons.

Change the Group

To apply this sort of change to more than one slide, hold down the Ctrl key and select as many slides as you want. Now click the Format menu and select Slide Layout. Pick a different layout, and the selected layout is applied to the group.

Change the Layout

The layout of the objects on any slide can be changed without affecting the other slides. Click on the placeholder. When it is selected, you can reposition it using the four-headed arrow pointer. You can also resize by pulling or dragging on the sizing handles at the corners and edges of the selection rectangle, just as you can with other graphic objects.

Color Changes

To change the> background color for just one slide, click the Format menu and select Background to open the Background dialog box. The drop-down list in the middle of the Background box displays the color scheme used in the template. You can choose More Colors or Fill Effects. To see how the change will look, click the Preview button. If you click the Apply button, the changes affect only the selected slide. If you want the changes to be shown on all the slides, you can click Apply to All.

From within the Background dialog box (see the preceding figure), choose Fill Effects to view several variations for background colors. The Gradients fill blends one or more colors and shades. Texture offers choices such as Woven mat and Water droplets. Pattern shows combinations of designs. The Picture tab enables you to use a piece of clip art as the background. This type of formatting is also available for AutoShapes. It is worthwhile to practice with these variations until you are familiar with the possibilities.

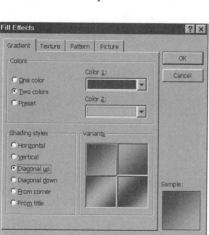

If you want to omit the background graphics that appear on the master, you can choose the check box on the lower-left corner of the Format, Background dialog box. The graphics can be omitted from just one slide or from the whole show by clicking either Apply, this slide only, or Apply to All, all the slides in the show.

Change a Single Element

To make changes to other objects on the slide, such as text and Fills, click the Format menu and select Slide Color Scheme to open the Color Scheme dialog box.

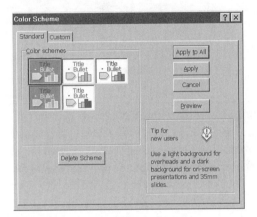

The Standard tab shows the basic color combinations for the selected design, including black and white.

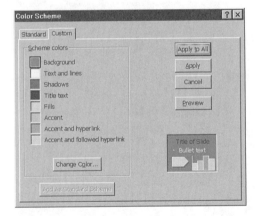

The Custom tab gives you the opportunity to change individual elements for one slide or for the whole show. These choices override the Design Master.

TAKE THE TEST

This task covers Objective 10, "Change the Order of Slides Using Slide Sorter View," and Objective 11, "Modify Slide Sequence in the Outline Pane." To begin this task, open the The Little General.ppt file from the CD.

Task 1

1. Move Slide 8 (Have I Got an Idea!) after Slide 2 (Creativity Session). Use the Slide Sorter view.

2. Move Slide 3 (Have I Got an Idea!) after Slide 1 using the Outline pane.

3. Save the file as C:\PP2000\Little Idea.ppt.

The solution file for this task is Ch03- Little Idea.ppt. To check your work, open Ch03- Little Idea.ppt. Then open your answer, C:\PP2000\Little Idea.ppt. Click Window on the Menu bar and choose Arrange All. The two shows will be displayed side by side.

This task covers Objective 12, "Change Slide Layout (Modify the Slide Master)"; Objective 13, "Insert Headers and Footers"; and Objective 14, "Change the Layout for One or More Slides." To begin this task, open the Small Thoughts file from the CD.

Task 2

1. On the Slide Master, change the Master title style to Arial.

2. Add General Sales Company to the footer on all the slides except the Title slides. Do not add the Date and time.

3. Change Slide 2 (Have I Got an Idea) to Title slide layout.

4. Save the file as C:\PP2000\Better Idea.ppt.

The solution file for this task is Ch03- Better Idea.ppt. To check your work, open Ch03- Better Idea.ppt. Then open your answer, C:\PP2000\Better Idea.ppt. Click Window on the Menu bar and choose Arrange All. The two shows will be displayed side by side.

Cheat Sheet

Change the Order of Slides

In ▦ Slide Sorter view, drag slides into any order.

Modify Slide Sequence in the Outline Pane

Drag the Title of the slide ahead of or below the target slide.

Change Slide Layout (Modify the Slide Master)

View, Master, Slide Master.

Or, hold Shift and click ▣ Slide view.

Insert Headers and Footers

View, Header and Footer

Change the Layout for One or More Slides

Select the slide. Format, Slide Layout.

To change more than one slide, select multiple slides with the Ctrl or Shift keys.

Working with Text

A picture might be worth a lot of words, but your presentation is bound to have text as well as graphics. Seven activities are covered in this chapter:

- Check Spelling

- Find and Replace Text

- Change and Replace Text Fonts (Individual Slide and Entire Presentation)

- Change the Text Alignment

- Use the Format Painter

- Enter Text in Tri-Pane View

- Promote and Demote Text in Slide and Outline Panes

PowerPoint 2000 uses the same tools as other Office applications. Many of the PowerPoint 2000 tools are less complex than the tools available in the other Office applications.

OBJECTIVE

15

Check Spelling

PowerPoint's spell checker works across all the elements of your presentation. It checks the spelling on notes and handouts, as well as on slides.

Automatic spell checking is on by default. If a word has a possible spelling error, a wavy red line appears under it.

Spelling flag ───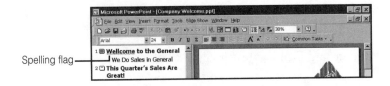

Automatic Spell Checking

The same proofing tools are used by all the other applications in Office 2000. When you right-click on the word, PowerPoint suggests an alternative if one is available. There are three methods to spell check the entire presentation:

- Click the Tools menu and select Spelling.

- Click ![ABC] Spelling on the Standard toolbar.

- Press F7.

A suggestion is given if one is available. You have the opportunity to correct that one instance of the word, or you can correct every occurrence by clicking the Change All button.

48

Find and Replace Text

One of the features of Microsoft applications is the set of common tools. If you have used Find and Replace in any other Microsoft program, you'll have no trouble here.

The Edit menu has a line item for Find and another for Replace. The dialog box that appears is simple. Just put the target text in the Find box and press Enter or click the Find Next button. You can choose to match the case of the text, or you can match a whole word only rather than just part of a word. The Find/Replace operation covers the entire presentation, including any note pages. The only view this won't work in, of course, is Slide Show.

Simple Find and Replace

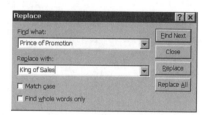

PowerPoint also uses the common keyboard shortcuts of Ctrl+F for Find and Ctrl+H for Replace.

17

Change and Replace Text Fonts (Individual Slide and Entire Presentation)

The terms *font* and *typeface* can loosely be used interchangeably. They refer to the look of the characters that are used in text. Fonts have different attributes, such as size, color, and appearance. PowerPoint enables you to change the fonts on just one slide or throughout the presentation.

View Formatting

You can change fonts in Outline view and then look at the slide itself to see the results. To see the text with formatting applied in Outline view, click ▣ Show Formatting on the Standard toolbar. When fonts are changed directly on the slide itself, you see the outcome immediately.

Change the Whole Show

To change fonts that are used in the whole presentation, click the Format menu and select Replace Fonts. If you have selected text, the dialog box suggests that typeface as the one that needs to be replaced.

You'll have to select each font that you want to replace.

If you want to set the text font for the entire presentation, click the <u>V</u>iew menu, point at <u>M</u>aster, and select <u>S</u>lide Master. You can work with the master by holding down the Shift key while clicking on the Slide View icon. Any changes that are made to the master are seen on every slide unless specific formatting has superceded that style.

To change the text fonts for an individual word, double-click the word or select it with the mouse. The changes affect only the selected word.

To select a line, click on the bullet or triple-click in the line.

If you want to apply changes to the entire text box, click on the border of the box. Any changes to a text box are applied to all the text in that box. Ctrl+A selects everything on a single slide so that all the text on a single slide can be changed.

The shortcut menu offers these same options. After the text or object that is to be changed has been selected, right-click to access the shortcut menu, and then choose <u>F</u>ont.

One Slide at a Time

18

Change the Text Alignment

The Formatting toolbar has three icons for aligning paragraphs to the left, right, or center.

Drag It

First, place the insertion point in the paragraph that is to be aligned. You do not have to select all the text. Now click on the appropriate icon, or click the Format menu and select Alignment to open the Format dialog box.

Alignment	Keyboard Shortcut	Toolbar Button	Uses
Left	Ctrl+L	▤	Most lides.
Center	Ctrl+E	▤	Headings and Titles.
Right	Ctrl+R	▤	For design layout reasons.
Justified	Ctrl+J		Newspaper-like columns. Not often used in Power-Point.

Ctrl+J justifies the paragraph, even though this shortcut does not appear on the menu. Full justification also does not appear as a default icon on the toolbar.

Another way to adjust the paragraph alignment is to use the ruler.

First select the text to be adjusted. A horizontal ruler should appear. If it does not, click the View menu and click Ruler. There are two indent markers on the ruler. The top one controls the first line of a paragraph. The bottom marker sets the indents for all the other lines. The lower marker has a square below it that enables you to change the indentation for the entire paragraph.

When there are bulleted items, you will see markers for each level of indentation.

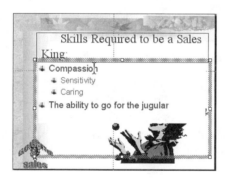

Use the Format Painter

When more than one formatting attribute has been applied to an object, such as a paragraph or an AutoShape, it's difficult to duplicate all those changes in another area. That's where the Format Painter comes in.

Select the Object

First, select the object that has the formatting you want to copy. Click ⬛ Format Painter on the Standard toolbar, and then select the object you want to format. You only have to place the insertion point in a paragraph to pick up the formatting.

Continue Painting

Double-click ⬛ Format Painter on the Standard toolbar to toggle the feature on. The Format Painter brush replaces the default pointer. It stays active so that more than one object can be formatted. When you're finished, click the icon once more to turn it off.

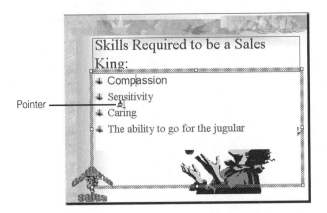

Pointer

Skills Required to be a Sales King:
- Compassion
- Sensitivity
- Caring
- The ability to go for the jugular

Enter Text in Tri-Pane View

PowerPoint shows three panes in Normal view. This tri-pane view gives you the opportunity to enter text directly on the slide or in the outline. You don't have to switch to Slide view to edit a slide.

When the insertion point is in one of the heading levels of the outline, the slide is shown to the right. Text can be directly entered in either pane. Whatever you type takes on the characteristics of that paragraph.

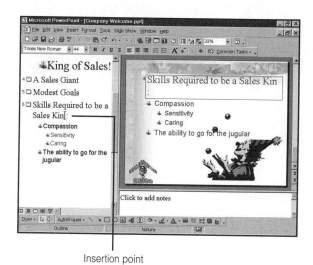

Insertion point

21

Promote and Demote Text in Slide and Outline Panes

A slide's title is a Heading 1 style—the top level of an outline. The subdivisions that follow the title are Heading 2, Heading 3, and so on. If a Heading 2 style is promoted to Heading 1, that text will be the title, and it becomes a new slide.

Use the Toolbar

The Formatting toolbar has an arrow icon to promote or demote text. You can promote text to a higher heading level by clicking on the ◀ Left arrow (Alt+Shift+Left), and you can demote text to a lower heading level with the ▶ Right arrow (Alt+Shift+Right). Select the text and click in the direction you want. This can be done in either Slide or Outline view.

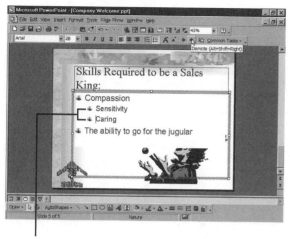

Demoted headings

If the insertion point is placed at the beginning of the text or between a bullet and the text, the text can also be promoted or demoted by using the Tab and Shift+Tab key. To actually insert a tab character, you can use Ctrl+Tab.

Keyboard Shortcuts

TAKE THE TEST

Task 1

This task covers Objective 15, "Check Spelling"; and Objective 16, "Find and Replace Text." To begin this task, open the Better Thoughts.ppt file from the CD.

Be careful with questions that ask you to replace words or fonts. Are they asking to have a word replaced on just one slide, or do they want it done to the whole show?

1. Spell check the presentation.

2. Replace the word *New* with the word *Better* throughout the presentation.

3. Change all the Times New Roman fonts to Arial.

4. Save the file as C:\PP2000\More Ideas.ppt.

The solution file for this task is Ch04-More Ideas.ppt. To check your work, open Ch04-More Ideas.ppt. Then open your answer, C:\PP2000\More Ideas.ppt. Click Window on the Menu bar and choose Arrange All. The two shows will be displayed side by side.

This task covers Objective 18, "Change the Text Alignment"; Objective 19, "Use the Format Painter"; Objective 20, "Enter Text in Tri-Pane View"; and Objective 21, "Promote and Demote Text in Slide and Outline Panes." To begin this task, open the More Thoughts file from the CD.

Task 2

1. On Slide 4 (Agenda), change the distance from the bullet to the text from 1/2 inch to 1 inch.

2. Go to Slide 7 (Rules). In tri-pane view, after "No idea is a bad idea," add a bullet that says, Blue sky thoughts are great.

3. After Be Creative, add a bullet that says, Anything goes, and after Take risks, add a bullet that says, No pain, no gain.

4. Demote, one level, "Blue sky thoughts are great," "Anything goes," and "No pain, no gain."

5. Make "Blue sky thoughts are great" bold and italic. Using the format painter, apply the same formatting to "Anything goes" and "No pain, no gain."

6. Save the file as C:\PP2000\General Ideas.ppt.

The solution file for this task is Ch04-General Ideas.ppt. To check your work, open Ch04-General Ideas.ppt. Then open your answer, C:\PP2000\General Ideas.ppt. Click Window on the Menu bar and choose Arrange All. The two shows will be displayed side by side.

Cheat Sheet

Check Spelling

Click ▦ Spelling or Tools, Spelling (F7).

Find and Replace Text

Edit, Find (Ctrl+F)

Edit, Replace (Ctrl+H)

Change and Replace Text Fonts

Format, Font, or right-click and choose Font.

Change fonts for the whole show using Format, Replace Fonts.

Change the Text Alignment

Format, Alignment

Or, on the Formatting toolbar,

▦	Left Justified	Ctrl+L
▦	Center	Ctrl+E
▦	Right Justified	Ctrl+R
▦	Justify	Ctrl+J

Use the Format Painter

1. Select the text or object whose formatting you want to copy.

2. ▦ Format Painter (double-click to format more than one object).

3. Click on the target text or object.

Enter Text in Tri-Pane View

Enter text in either Outline or Slide pane. Text can also be entered in the Notes pane in this view.

Cheat Sheet

Promote and Demote Text in Slide and Outline Panes

⬅ Promote (Alt+Shift+Left) or

➡ Demote (Alt+Shift+Right)

More Ways to Work with Text

Four more text activities are expected on the exam. Practice drawing text boxes and adding text to shapes. Make sure you know how to wrap text within a shape. Importing text from Word is an easy way to create content in a PowerPoint show—there is bound to be at least one question about importing Word text.

The only item in this group that is new with Office 2000 is the Office Clipboard. If the Clipboard toolbar doesn't appear automatically, be sure you know how to turn it on.

- Create a Text Box for Entering Text
- Use the Wrap Text in AutoShape Feature
- Use the Office Clipboard
- Import Text from Word

22

Create a Text Box for Entering Text

PowerPoint slides are composed of graphic and text objects. The text on a slide is contained in a text box. A common layout for a slide consists of two text boxes: one for the title and another for the body text.

Draw It

On a blank presentation slide, follow these steps to draw a text box:

1. Select ▣ Text Box on the Draw toolbar, or select the Insert menu and click Te_x_t Box to change the pointer to a dagger.

2. Position this dagger approximately where you want to place a text box.

3. Continue holding down the left button, and drag a box as wide as you think you want it.

When the mouse button is released, a box appears with your specified width, but just one line high. The insertion point will be flashing inside. When you draw a box, the text wraps, making the box taller as more text is entered.

If you click in just one spot with the dagger pointer, the text does not wrap.

To format the text box, click the border of the Text box with the right mouse button. The Shortcut menu gives you the opportunity to change the Font or choose Format Text Box to add a border or to change the flow of the text.

Right-click the mouse to bring up a shortcut menu.

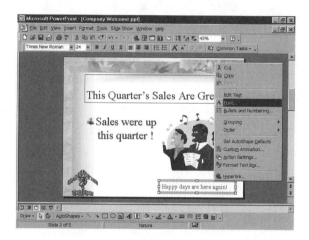

23

Use the Wrap Text in AutoShape Feature

To add text to an AutoShape, choose the object and start typing. Text added in this way does not wrap. It does not restrict itself to the outline of the shape.

Mold the Shape

1. Select the AutoShape with unwrapped text.

2. Click the Format menu and choose AutoShape, or right-click the mouse on the AutoShape.

3. Click on the Text Box tab.

You can now choose to have the text wrap to fit the outline of the AutoShape, or have the AutoShape resize to fit the text.

Resizing enlarges or shrinks the object to fit the text.

Fitting the AutoShape retains the size of the object, but excess text will flow beyond the borders of the object.

There are other choices on the Text Box tab, including where the text will anchor itself in relation to the object. You can define the distance between the borders of the object and the text using the Internal margin options. Text can also be rotated by 90 degrees. The exam probably won't go into this much detail, but it is worthwhile to be aware of these items, just in case.

To place an AutoShape, select AutoShape on the Drawing toolbar and drag a shape to a Presentation page.

24

Use the Office Clipboard

The Office Clipboard is available only in PowerPoint, Word, Excel, Access, and Outlook. Outside these applications is still the regular Windows Clipboard.

New with Office 2000 is the Office Clipboard. The new clipboard can hold up to 12 items. You can choose which of these items to paste.

The Office Clipboard can be accessed by clicking View and then choosing Toolbars, Clipboard, or by clicking the right mouse button on any toolbar and choosing Clipboard. If you copy two objects without using Paste in between, the Clipboard toolbar appears (if PowerPoint 2000 is your active window). Be aware that other windows might obscure the Office Clipboard.

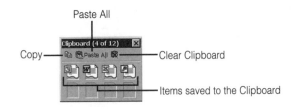

Paste All

Copy — Clear Clipboard

Items saved to the Clipboard

The second row of the toolbar shows the items being held on the Clipboard. The item icons reflect the type of object that was copied, for example picture or text. An exam question might possibly ask you to copy more than one item and then paste the items in another location.

To tell one item from another, rest the pointer over an item. The first 50 characters of copied text are displayed when the pointer rests on the item. Pictures are numbered in the order in which they were copied. To paste an individual item, click it on the Clipboard. To Paste all the items on the Clipboard, click the Paste All button. Issuing the Undo Paste command after pasting multiple items backs out pasted objects, one at a time.

The Clipboard floats by default but can be docked like any other toolbar. If the Clipboard toolbar is docked, you see a drop-down arrow next to the word Items. When this is clicked, you can see all the items that are on the Clipboard.

25

Import Text from Word

The text in a Word document can be brought in as either text on a slide or as an outline for a presentation.

To add the contents of an entire Word file to a slide, click the Insert menu and select Object. Choose Create from File, and then Browse to locate the document. If the Link box is selected, any changes made to the document later will be picked up by the presentation.

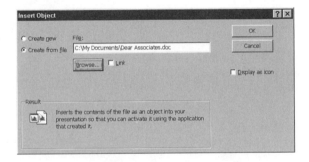

To edit the document, double-click the object. A linked object will jump back to the original document, and an unlinked object will display Word toolbars and menus.

If you want only part of a document, you can copy and paste the selection on a slide. Click the Edit menu, click Paste Special, and select Paste link to make sure the text is updated when the original document is edited.

A new presentation can be created from a Word outline. First access the Open dialog box using one of the following methods:

- Click the File menu and select Open.

- Click ⬛ Open on the Standard toolbar.

- Press Ctrl+O.

On the drop-down list for Files of type, you will find an entry for All Outlines. PowerPoint can create a show from .txt, .xls, and other formats as well as from Word .doc files. Find the file you want to use and click Open.

When PowerPoint imports text, it uses heading styles to create slides. Heading 1 produces a slide. Lower-level headings, such as Heading 2 or 3, fill in the text on a slide. If styles are not used, PowerPoint uses tab settings to put together an outline.

Follow these steps to add the Word text to an existing presentation:

1. Place your insertion point in the Outline pane where you want the new information added.

2. Click the Insert menu and select Slides from Outline.

3. The All Outlines selection should show in the Files of type drop-down list. Select the file and click on the Insert button.

TAKE THE TEST

Task 1

This task covers Objective 22, "Create a Text Box for Entering Text." Open the Simple Thoughts file from the CD to begin this task.

1. Draw a text box that is four inches wide in the center of slide 11.

2. Insert the text General Sales Brainstorming Session. Make the font Bold, Arial, 44 points. Center the text. Adjust the box to stack the text in three lines: General Sales, Brainstorming, and Session.

3. Save the file as C:\PP2000\One idea.ppt.

The solution file for this task is Ch05-One Idea.ppt. To check your work, open Ch05-One Idea.ppt. Then open your answer, C:\PP2000\One Idea.ppt. Click Window on the Menu bar and choose Arrange All. The two shows will be displayed side by side.

Task 2

This task covers Objective 23, "Use the Wrap Text in AutoShape Feature"; and Objective 25, "Import Text from Word." Open the Second Thoughts file from the CD to begin this task.

1. On Slide 9, make the text wrap to fit the Auto shape.

2. On Slide 10, insert a Word document named Thank You.doc in the practice lab. Deselect the object.

3. Save the file as C:\PP2000\Two Ideas.ppt.

The solution file for this task is Ch05-Two Ideas.ppt. To check your work, open Ch05-Two Ideas.ppt. Then open your answer, C:\PP2000\Two Ideas.ppt. Click <u>W</u>indow on the Menu bar and choose <u>A</u>rrange All. The two shows will be displayed side by side.

This task covers Objective 24, "Use the Office Clipboard." Open the General Thoughts file to begin this task.

Task 3

1. Use the Office Clipboard to copy the figures in the lower-right corners of slides 4, 5, 6, 7, and 8.

2. Paste the figures on slide 9. Arrange the figures, one in each corner and one in the middle of the slide. They don't have to be in any particular order.

3. Save the file as C:\PP2000\Simple Ideas.ppt.

The solution file for this task is Ch05-Simple Ideas.ppt. To check your work, open Ch05-Simple Ideas.ppt. Then open your answer, C:\PP2000\Simple Ideas.ppt. Click <u>W</u>indow on the Menu bar and choose <u>A</u>rrange All. The two shows will be displayed side by side.

Cheat Sheet

Create a Text Box for Entering Text

Insert, Text Box

Use the Wrap Text in AutoShape Feature

1. Format, AutoShape.

2. Click on the Text Box tab.

3. Choose Word wrap text in AutoShape or Resize AutoShape to fit text.

The right mouse context menu brings up the same options.

Use the Office Clipboard

1. Open the Clipboard:

   - View, Toolbars, Clipboard

   - Right-click any toolbar, Clipboard

2. Click the icon for the item you want to paste, or Paste All to paste every item.

Import Text from Word

1. Insert, Object.

2. Choose Create from file.

New show:

1. File, Open (Ctrl+O).

2. Choose All Outlines.

Add slides to existing show:

1. Place insertion point in existing outline.

2. Insert, Slides from Outline.

3. Select the file and click on the Insert button.

Working with Visual Elements

Graphics, pictures, and shapes are important in PowerPoint. You will be asked to insert particular AutoShapes, such as a 5-point Star or a Left-Right Arrow. After you have placed objects on a slide, you might be asked to group or combine figures. You might also be asked to insert a particular graphic from the Clip Gallery. Following are the activities covered in this chapter:

- Add a Picture from the Clip Gallery

- Add and Group Shapes Using WordArt or the Drawing Toolbar

- Rotate and Fill an Object

26

Add a Picture from the Clip Gallery

Office 2000 uses the latest version of Clip Gallery, a cataloging tool that organizes Clip Art. The new Clip Gallery can even be run as a standalone application.

Open the Gallery

The Draw bar has an icon that you can use to Insert Clip Art ▣. Another way to bring up the Gallery is to click the Insert menu, select Picture, and then select Clip Art. If the slide you are working on has a Clip Art placeholder, the Gallery opens when you double-click the icon.

Initially, about 50 categories are displayed. If you know the category, click on it. The available Clip Art is displayed in a miniature form.

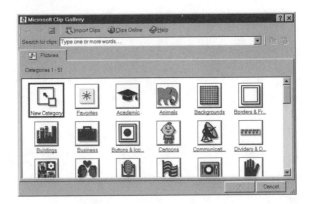

Clicking with the right mouse button brings up a context menu. Select a graphic by clicking the left mouse button; this provides you with four options.

When you pause the cursor over a picture, the name and size of the graphic are displayed.

Preview clip   Insert clip

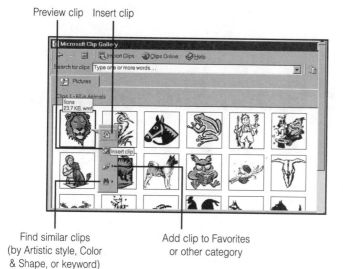

Find similar clips
(by Artistic style, Color
& Shape, or keyword)

Add clip to Favorites
or other category

The box does not close after you pick Insert Clip; you must do that yourself. The right mouse button gives you some other choices, such as copy, paste, and a detailed look at the clip's properties.

When the image is placed on a slide, it can be dragged to other locations or resized. This is covered in Objectives 27 and 29.

OBJECTIVE

27

Add and Group Shapes Using WordArt or the Drawing Toolbar

A collection of shapes is included with PowerPoint: stars, arrows, flowchart objects, and others. You can also format text into dramatic shapes using WordArt.

Both WordArt and AutoShapes are on the Draw toolbar. If you don't see the toolbar, go to View, Toolbars, and check Drawing.

AutoShapes To insert an AutoShape, click on the AutoShape icon on the toolbar and choose the shape you want from the various groups.

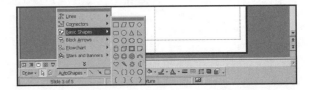

When the desired shape is selected, the pointer changes to a cross. Position the pointer approximately where you want to place the object, and click. The shape is inserted and can be resized. To more closely insert a shape in the desired size, drag out a shape to the size you want after selecting from the AutoShape menu. Holding down the Shift key keeps the shape's ratio of height and width.

78

WordArt creates an object from text. You can create WordArt in two ways:

WordArt

- Click 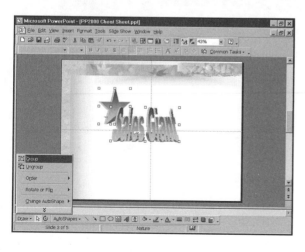 WordArt on the Drawing toolbar, and the wizard will walk you through the process. First choose a style from the WordArt Gallery and click OK. Next, type the desired text in the WordArt text and click OK. The OK button drops the WordArt object onto the slide so that it can be moved to the appropriate spot.

- You can also select text that is already on the slide for WordArt to use. Clicking on WordArt creates an object with the previously selected text but does not remove the original text. When selecting text, you must be sure to select the text itself, not just the text box.

You can use grouping to create new items from two or more separate objects. You might want to add a WordArt figure to an AutoShape or combine two shapes to make a unique figure.

Grouping

To group Draw objects, AutoShapes, or WordArt figures, first select each object. If the Shift key is held down, you can select the objects to be grouped. Another way to select objects that are close together is to use the pointer to draw a box around the objects; all objects inside the box will be selected. Next, click Draw on the toolbar and choose Group from the menu. If Group is grayed out, you might have included a placeholder.

After objects are grouped, they can be moved and formatted as if they were a single item.

28

Rotate and Fill an Object

Objects can be rotated around their centers or corners. You can also flip an object horizontally or vertically.

Spin the Shape

Click on the object to select it. Now click  Free Rotate on the Drawing toolbar. You can drag the corners of the object to any angle you choose by using the Free Rotate handles at the corners of the object.

Free Rotate handles

When the object is in the position you want, click outside the object to fix its position. The object moves in 15-degree angles if you hold down the Shift key. To rotate around the corner opposite the handle you're using, hold down the Ctrl key.

To precisely rotate an object, select the object and click the Format menu. Select the object from the menu; the Size tab enables you to specify the exact degree of rotation. The menu selection changes depending on the type of object selected.

To change the fill color of an object, select it and click on the arrow next to  Fill Color on the Drawing toolbar.

Change Color

No Fill	The object will be transparent.
Automatic	A selection of colors that make up the color scheme for the selected template. The ToolTip that appears when the pointer rests on a color tells you what that color is intended for.
More Fill Colors	This choice enables you to customize the slide with colors other than those that are part of the color scheme.
Fill Effects	Many combinations are possible here, from gradations of color to inserted pictures.

TAKE THE TEST

This task covers Objective 26, "Add a Picture from the Clip Gallery." Open the Great Thoughts file from the enclosed CD to begin this task.

1. Select blank slide number 9.

2. Locate and insert the image of the ringmaster from ClipArt. The Key word is Ringmasters (it's the same picture that appears on the title slide).

3. Using the second WordArt style from the left on the top row of the WordArt Gallery dialog box, insert the phrase Welcome All!.

4. Select both the WordArt object and the Clip Art. Group the two and move the group to the lower-right corner of the slide.

5. Use AutoShapes to add a 4-point star to the slide. Make the star about 4 inches wide and 4 inches tall.

6. Fill the star with a Gradient Fill effect, using the default orange and shading from center.

7. Rotate the star to the right so that the horizontal arms are pointing toward the Clip Art.

8. Save the file as C:\PP2000\Great Ideas.ppt.

The solution file for this task is Ch06-Great Ideas.ppt. To check your work, open Ch06-Great Ideas.ppt. Then open your answer, C:\PP2000\Great Ideas.ppt. Click Window on the Menu bar and choose Arrange All. The two shows will be displayed side by side.

Cheat Sheet

Add a Picture from the Clip Gallery

- on the Drawing toolbar.

- Insert, Picture, Clip Art.

- Double-click the placeholder icon.

Add and Group Shapes Using WordArt or the Drawing Toolbar

Click the AutoShape or on the Drawing toolbar.

Rotate and Fill an Object

- Free Rotate on the Drawing toolbar.

- Fill Color on the Drawing toolbar.

- Format, Object, Size, Rotation.

More on Formatting and Graphics

Three objectives covered in this chapter relate to AutoShapes and ClipArt. You can be asked to insert pictures or shapes and then arrange them on the slide. AutoShapes can also be dressed up with borders, shadows, colors, and 3D formatting.

The fourth task involves working with tables—creating tables and adding, deleting, and merging cells.

- Scale and Size an Object Including ClipArt
- Place Text Inside a Shape Using a Text Box
- Apply Formatting
- Create Tables Within PowerPoint

OBJECTIVE

29

Scale and Size an Object Including ClipArt

An object, including ClipArt, can be resized to fit the purpose or layout.

Drag to Size

You can select an object and then drag the boundary handles of an object to resize it. Drag the handles at the corners while holding down the Shift key to resize with height and width remaining in proportion. Hold down the Shift key to create squares or circles rather than rectangles or ovals.

If you hold down the Ctrl key while dragging the handle, the object will keep its position on the page while you change the size.

Exact Dimensions

There are times when you will want to scale or resize an object to a definite amount. After selecting the object, click the Format menu or right-click the object. The menu will change depending on the item selected: AutoShape, Placeholder, Picture, and so on. The Size tab includes options for Height, Width, and Rotation that you can specify. Scale, the lower half of the dialog box, will accept percentage figures to resize the item. If you want to maintain the height/width ratio, check the Lock aspect ration box.

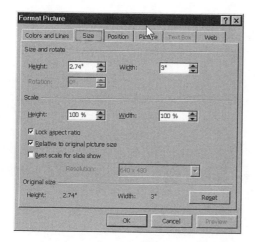

You'll find two other check boxes when you click the Format menu, select Object, and then click Size; these are the Relative to original picture size check box and the Best scale for a slide show check box. These options are for pictures or ClipArt only. They are not available for other elements such as a drawn rectangle or AutoShape object.

Relative to original picture size keeps the height and width percentages in the scale based on the original size of the ClipArt. Without this option, the picture will be scaled based on its present size.

Best scale for slide show adjusts the picture to be best seen depending on the resolution of your monitor.

Other Check Boxes

30

Place Text Inside a Shape Using a Text Box

There are two ways to apply text to an object. One makes the text a part of the shape, so that it can be sized and rotated with the object. Objective 23, "Use the Wrap Text in AutoShape Feature," deals with adding text directly to an object.

The other technique treats text independently by inserting it in a text box, separate from the shape.

For the exam, make sure you know the difference.

Separate Text

If you don't want the text to be part of the object, you can create a holder by clicking ▣ Text Box on the Drawing toolbar. The pointer changes to a dagger, allowing you to draw a box and place it on top of the shape. Text created this way will not rotate with the object unless the object and the text box are grouped. See Objective 27, "Add and Group Shapes Using WordArt or the Drawing Toolbar."

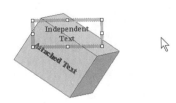

If you need to add independent text to a shape, select the object and start typing. The text will be attached to the object and can be formatted to fit. Note that not all objects will support attached text. Follow these steps to add independent text to a shape:

1. Select the object.

2. Click the Format menu, and select Object.

3. Click the Text Box tab. One of the options on this tab enables you to choose the Text anchor point or position in the shape. Other choices include Word wrap text in AutoShape, which keeps the text inside the shape, or Resize AutoShape to fit text, which fits the shape to the size of the text.

31

Apply Formatting

When inserted in a slide, AutoShapes take on the defaults displayed in Format, Slide Color Scheme. Individual elements can be reformatted using dialog boxes from menu items or the icons available on the Drawing toolbar.

On the exam, you will be asked to format an item; it will be specific. For example, it might call for applying a Shadow Style 6. You can determine the names of the styles by letting the pointer rest over the icon.

Through the Format Dialog

You can edit the formatting attributes of objects by selecting the object and clicking the Format menu. Different items display depending on the object.

There are six tabs on the Format Dialog box

Tab	Description
Colors and Lines	The Color and Lines tab provides another way to select the fill color of an object. Besides Fill Color, you can also make the object Semitransparent. The Style of the border or line around an object can be made thick, dashed, or of a different Color and Weight or point size.
Size	The dimensions of the object can be precisely determined on the Size tab. See Objective 29.

Tab	Description
Position	This area enables you to set the object's position in relation to the Top-Left Corner or the Center of the slide.
Picture	The first option on this tab provides a means of precisely cropping a picture. Image control can adjust the color, brightness, and contrast of a picture. You can change a picture to grayscale or dim the colors like a watermark.
Text Box	If the element is a text box, this tab is used to set exact positioning and text alignment preferences.
Web	The Web tab is used to insert the alternative text that will be seen if a reader has turned pictures off in his browser. This text will also appear when a pointer rests on an object while using Internet Explorer 4.0 or Netscape 4.0 and above.

From the Toolbar

Other formatting options exist on the Drawing toolbar. An icon that displays a drop-down arrow, such as 🖌 Fill color, will use the default setting or the last one selected. To change the setting, click the drop-down arrow and choose an alternative.

Some icons have no drop-down list, such as 🔲 Shadow. When you click on one of these icons, a list will appear. These icons do not immediately apply formatting; you must first make a selection.

In the following list, *Default* means that the default or last used formatting will be applied. Use the arrow on the right to change the setting. *List* means that a choice must be made before the object is formatted.

	Fill Color	Internal color of an object	Default
	Line Color	Border color	Default
	Font Color	Text color	Default
	Line Style	Line thickness	List
	Dash Style	Dashes and dots	List
	Arrow Style	Direction and arrow heads	List
	Shadow	Behind, in front, or angled	List
	3D	Extrusion size and direction	Default

For information about the Format Painter, see Objective 19.

Create Tables Within PowerPoint

PowerPoint now enables you to create tables without having to import them from Word or Excel. Tables provide a convenient way to place text and graphics on the slide. It's easier to use than trying to place objects using the Tab key and spacebar.

You can insert a table using either the Insert menu or the Standard toolbar. To insert a table using the Insert menu, follow these steps:

Insert a Table

1. Click the Insert menu and select Table. You will be given a dialog box to select the number of columns and rows.

2. Enter the required number of columns and rows.

To insert a table by using the Standard toolbar, follow these steps:

1. Click ▦ Insert Table on the Standard toolbar. A dialog box with a grid will appear.

2. Drag the pointer over the squares. As you do so, you will see the dimensions on the bottom of the dialog box.

3. You can pass the pointer over the cells to select the range, and then click the left button, or you can hold down the left button and a table will appear when you release it.

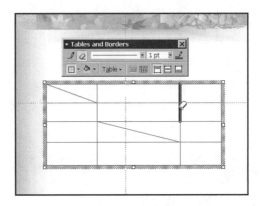

The table will appear in the middle of the slide. It can be moved or resized like any other graphic element.

Use the Tables and Borders Toolbar

There is a toolbar devoted to tables; click the View menu, select Toolbars, and then click Tables and Borders.

The Table and Borders toolbar can be used to format a table. First, select one cell, and place the insertion point in that square. To select more than one, drag across the desired squares.

On the Tables and Borders toolbar:

- Merge Cells combines two or more selected cells into one. The text will be combined in the upper-left cell.

- Split Cells divides the cell in two.

- Alignment options for Top Center and Bottom enables you to align text in relation to the top of the cell.

- Draw Table pen icon is used to split cells. Click this pen to make it active. Click the icon a second time to turn it off. You can draw horizontal, vertical, or diagonal lines that will split the cells.

Eraser merges adjacent cells. Click the eraser once to turn it on, and click it a second time to deactivate it. Use this tool to erase lines between cells or to merge adjacent cells.

TAKE THE TEST

Task 1

This task covers Objective 29, "Scale and Size an Object Including ClipArt"; Objective 30, "Place Text Inside a Shape Using a Text Box"; and Objective 31, "Apply Formatting." To begin this task, open the Little Thought file from the CD.

1. Insert a new blank slide before slide 3.

2. Insert an AutoShape of a Horizontal Scroll banner on the new slide 3.

3. Size the object to 6 inches high and 7 inches wide. Place the left edge of the Shape about 3.5 inches left of the center of the slide.

4. Place a text box on the banner with the text Notes will be available at the back of the room in Arial, bold, 36 points. Center the text.

5. Make the text box fill dark blue and the font white.

6. Format the banner with the default light blue Gradient fill from the center.

7. Deselect the objects.

8. Save the file as C:\PP2000\Major Idea.ppt.

The solution file for this task is Ch7-Major Idea.ppt. To check your work, open Ch7- Major Idea.ppt. Then open your answer: C:\PP2000\ Major Idea.ppt. Click Window on the menu bar and choose Arrange All. The two shows will be displayed side by side. Directions for the task are in Objectives 29–31.

This task covers Objective 32, "Create Tables Within PowerPoint." To begin this task, open the Little Thought file from the CD.

1. Insert a 6×6 table on Slide 4.

2. Use the Eraser to make just one cell in the top row.

3. Type the word Schedule in the cell and center the text vertically and horizontally.

4. Deselect the table.

5. Save the file as C:\PP2000\Minor Idea.ppt.

The solution file for this task is Ch7-Minor Idea.ppt. To check your work, open Ch7- Minor Idea.ppt. Then open your answer: C:\PP2000\ Minor Idea.ppt. Click Window on the menu bar and choose Arrange All. The two shows will be displayed side by side. Directions for the task are in Objective 32.

Cheat Sheet

Scale and Size an Object Including ClipArt

Select object, drag boundary boxes.

1. Select object.
2. Format, Object (AutoShape, Placeholder, Picture).
3. Choose the Size tab.

Place Text Inside a Shape Using a Text Box

📧 on the Drawing toolbar Draw a box or click on slide and start typing.

Apply Formatting

1. Select object.
2. Format, Object (AutoShape, Placeholder, Picture).

See icon list in Objective 31.

Create Tables Within PowerPoint

- Insert, Table
- 📊 Tables and Borders Toolbar icon
- ✏️ Draw Table pen
- 🔲 Insert Table icon

Customizing a Presentation

PowerPoint has a variety of ways to put a slide show together that will fit your particular needs. Five of these activities are covered here:

- Add AutoNumber Bullets
- Add Graphical Bullets
- Add Slide Transitions
- Animate Text and Objects
- Add Speaker Notes

Add AutoNumber Bullets

Setting up an ordered or numbered list has been made easy in PowerPoint.

Start Numbering

The quickest way is to select the existing list you want to number and click ▦ Numbered List on the Formatting toolbar. You can also select the placeholder and then ▦ Numbered List to accomplish the same thing.

Click the Format menu and select Bullets and Numbering to see a choice of bullets or numbering.

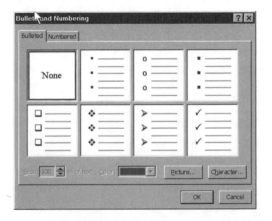

You also can set up a numbered list in a text box by typing a number (1, A, a or Roman numeral I) followed by either a period or a closing parenthesis mark. Type the text and press

Enter. The following lines will be automatically numbered each time you press the Enter key.

To stop AutoNumber or Bullets, either press the Backspace key or click ▤ Numbered List on the Formatting toolbar.

Stop Numbering

Add Graphical Bullets

An AutoLayout on the New Slide template has a bulleted list as its placeholder. You can also click Bullets on the toolbar, but after awhile these plain font type bullets become passé. PowerPoint allows graphical bullets as well; on the test you will be expected to know how to find and place them on your slide.

Choose Fancy Bullets

Select the text with the bullets you would like to change or add. You can also choose the placeholder itself. Click the Format menu and select Bullets and Numbering. At the bottom of the Bulleted Tab of the dialog box are two buttons. The Character button will let you choose a different character or font to use for bullets. The Picture button will let you substitute a graphical bullet.

Clip Gallery will appear if it was installed. Otherwise, it will display Insert Picture. Choose any of the included bullets. A callout menu will appear with three choices: Insert Clip, Preview the Clip, or Search for Similar Files. If you choose Insert Clip, the bullet will be substituted for the existing version and will be used when you add new items to the list.

Add Slide Transitions

How PowerPoint displays the change from one slide to another is called *Slide Transitions*. The default is No Transition, which advances to the next slide without any special effects. On the exam you might be asked to change the transition.

Transitions can be set up or edited in any view except when the presentation is running in Slide Show view. To create a transition, Click the Slide Show menu and select Slide Transition.

Make Changes

When you are in Slide Sorter view, Click ⬚ Slide Transition on the Slide Sorter toolbar, or select a transition from the Slide Transition Effects drop-down box on the Slide Sorter toolbar. (In Slide Sorter view, the right mouse context menu includes Slide Transition.)

There are 42 variations, including Random Transitions and No Transition. No Transition is a change to the next slide without any special effects. The preview picture will display what the transition will look like.

Choose a New Transition

There are three options for transition speed: Slow, Medium, and Fast. You can choose to Advance the slide On a mouse click or Automatically after a specified length of time. Sounds can also be played when the slide changes.

The choices made in this dialog box can Apply to All slides in the show or the transition can Apply to the selected slide(s) alone.

When a transition format is applied to a slide, you will see a small slide with an arrow icon in Sorter view.

Animate Text and Objects

In Normal, Outline, or Slide view, individual items can be selected and animated. It's probably best to work in Slide view because the objects appear larger.

Select an object and click the right mouse button. One of the items on that shortcut menu is Custo<u>m</u> Animation. Click the Sli<u>d</u>e Show menu and select Custo<u>m</u> Animation to make the same selection.

Choose a Motion

PowerPoint 2000 makes it easy to set up animation. Each object on the slide is listed with a check box next to its name.

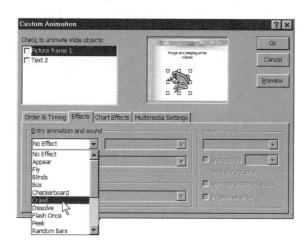

On the Custom Animation dialog box, a preview picture shows which object has been selected. On the Effects tab, the action is selected first, and then the attribute can be selected.

You can choose a sound to play when the object is animated. When the animation is finished, the object can be dimmed or changed to a different color. Other options include hiding the object either after the animation or the next time the mouse is clicked.

Determine the Order

The order in which the objects are animated can be determined on the Order & Timing tab. The other tabs provide animations for charts and movies or sound. The later two tabs are active only if the appropriate object is selected. A Preview button permits the designer to look at the animation without having to run the whole show.

Add Speaker Notes

Speaker notes are easily produced in Normal view. The Notes pane at the bottom of the screen can be resized if needed.

Click the View menu and select Notes Page to display the Notes Page itself with a picture of the current slide.

Open the Notes Page

If you want to add pictures or drawing objects to the speaker's notes, click the View menu and select Notes Page. The object will not be seen in the Normal or Outline view of the Notes pane.

Add Pictures

During a slide show, you can access the speaker's notes by right-clicking the slide. Notes can be sent to Word for more formatting options. You can also use the notes to produce a Web presentation with notes below each slide as an explanation.

Click the right mouse button while you are on the Notes Page. The shortcut menu offers several ways to format the speaker notes.

Format Speaker Notes

TAKE THE TEST

Task 1

This task covers Objective 33, "Add AutoNumber Bullets"; and
Objective 34, "Add Graphical Bullets." To begin this task, open
the Minor Thoughts file from the CD.

> **1.** Apply numbering to the list on Slide 4 (Agenda). Add a
> fifth item, coffee.
>
> **2.** Go to Slide 7 (Rules) and change the bullets to Graphical
> bullets. Use the third picture on the top row.
>
> **3.** Save the file as `C:\PP2000\New Idea.ppt`.

The solution file for this task is Ch08-New Idea.ppt. To check
your work, open Ch08- New Idea.ppt. Then open your answer:
C:\PP2000\ New Idea.ppt. Click <u>W</u>indow on the menu bar
and choose <u>A</u>rrange All. The two shows will be displayed side
by side. Directions for the task are in Objectives 33 and 34.

Task 2

This task covers Objective 35, "Add Slide Transitions";
Objective 36, "Animate Text and Objects"; and Objective 37,
"Add Speaker Notes." To begin this task, open the New
Thought file from the CD.

> **1.** Create a speaker's note for Slide 1. "General information
> slides follow Slide #9."
>
> **2.** Apply animation to the Clip Art objects in the lower-right
> corners of Slides 5, 6, 7, 8, and 9. Apply Stretch from the
> bottom to each object.

3. Put a random slide transition on all the slides. Slides are to advance on mouse click.

4. Save the file as C:\PP2000\Old Idea.ppt.

The solution file for this task is Ch08-Old Idea.ppt. To check your work, open Ch08-Show Ideas.ppt. Then open your answer: C:\PP2000\Old Idea.ppt. Click Window on the menu

Cheat Sheet

bar and choose <u>A</u>rrange All. The two shows will be displayed side by side. Directions for the task are in Objectives 35–37.

Add AutoNumber Bullets

Select the text or placeholder

▤ F<u>o</u>rmat, <u>B</u>ullets, and Numbering

Add Graphical Bullets

F<u>o</u>rmat, <u>B</u>ullets, and Numbering. <u>P</u>icture.

Add Slide Transitions

▥ Sli<u>d</u>e Show, Slide <u>T</u>ransition

Select transition from Slide Transition Effects on the Slide Sorter toolbar.

Right-click slide in Slide Sorter view. Choose Slide <u>T</u>ransition.

Animate Text and Objects

1. Select an object.

2. Right-click the object, Custo<u>m</u> Animation

   or click Sli<u>d</u>e Show, Custo<u>m</u> Animation

Add Speaker Notes

<u>V</u>iew, Notes <u>P</u>age.

Add text to Notes pane in Normal or Outline view.

Creating Output

This skill set could have been titled "How to Print Your Slide Show." The exam will have alternative ways to handle printing. You won't be using a physical printer, but the process should not throw you if you follow the directions.

Some of these tasks, such as preview in black and white, cannot be saved with a file. In such cases, be very careful to follow the instructions word for word. The "testing engine" can tell whether you have followed directions. It is important in these circumstances that you leave the screen so that your work is visible.

- Preview Presentation in Black and White
- Print Slides in a Variety of Formats
- Print Audience Handouts
- Print Speaker Notes in a Specified Format
- Print a Slide as an Overhead Transparency

38

Preview Presentation in Black and White

If you plan to print out your show on a black-and-white printer, PowerPoint has a way to preview the output.

Black and White Mock-Up

There are several ways to look at slides in grayscale or in pure black and white. To preview the slide in grayscale, click on ☑ Grayscale Preview on the Standard toolbar. To preview the slide in pure black and white, click on the Pure Black and White Preview icon on the Standard toolbar while holding down the Shift key. Or, click the View menu and select Black and White to see slides in black and white.

Another method of previewing the slide is to open the slide in Normal or Slide View, click on the Grayscale Preview button, and then right-click the slide. Select Black and White from the shortcut menu. A variety of choices of pure black and white and gray shades are listed. Click the desired option. To preview an object contained in the slide, right-click the object and select Black and White from the shortcut menu. Click on the desired option.

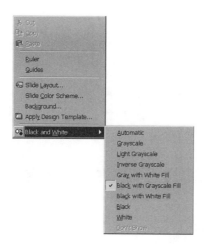

High Contrast is a feature that improves screen readability with high-contrast colors and easily readable fonts. It can be selected through Accessibility options on the control panel. When High Contrast is selected, PowerPoint menus, toolbars, and panes are displayed in high-contrast black and white. To make the slides display in high-contrast black and white, click on the High Contrast Black and White icon. High Contrast can be seen only on the screen—it is not a printing option.

39

Print Slides in a Variety of Formats

You can print either the whole show or individual slides in various forms.

Choose Print Objects

Click the File menu and select Print for a choice of items to print:

- Slides
- Handouts
- Notes pages
- Outline view

The Outline printout will include all the text formatting, even if you had it hidden in Outline or Normal view.

If you choose to print out the slides, they can be printed

- In Pure black and white
- Grayscale
- Scaled to fit the paper
- Framed

The Send to option on the File menu gives you the opportunity to send the presentation to Word for further formatting, editing, and printing. You can also use Send to to prepare the slides to be sent to a service bureau to be prepared as 35mm slides, overheads, posters, and so on. Slides can also be routed to others for review or posted to Microsoft Exchange public folders. System requirements and options might vary depending on the email program being used.

File, Page Setup has provisions for setting up the size of the slides for 35mm slides, banners, onscreen show, overhead, or paper. Portrait and Landscape settings are available for slides, notes, handouts, and outlines. The Number Slides From box enables you to change the starting slide number.

Print Audience Handouts

**Audience
Handouts**

Click the File menu and select Print. Drop down the list under Print what and choose Handouts. The Handouts section of the Print box becomes available, and you can select the number of slides to print on a page, the order, and whether they are Horizontal or Vertical. You can choose from two to nine slides per page.

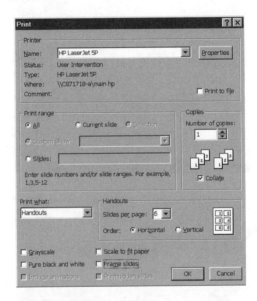

To change the layout of Handouts, click the View menu, select Master, and choose Handout Master. You can insert header and footer material, or you can place graphics (such as your company logo) on the Handout page. Items that are added appear only on the handouts; the slide master is not changed.

41 OBJECTIVE

Print Speaker Notes in a Specified Format

Speaker notes display a miniature slide and the text that is placed in the Notes pane or entered in Notes view.

The Notes Master layout can be edited. Click the View menu, select Master, and then choose Notes Master. Notes are displayed onscreen if your presentation is saved as a Web page.

There are more formatting options in Word, so you might want to edit your notes in Word. To send the notes to Word, click the File menu and select Send to. When you choose to send the PowerPoint show to Microsoft Word, you are shown a Write-Up dialog box.

The File, Send to option offers five page layout options, plus the capability to link the slides so that changes are reflected in the Word document. You can choose to have the notes displayed in the document or to have Word produce blank lines next to or below the slides.

Use PowerPoint or Word

There are no lines on the PowerPoint handouts. To provide blank lines to help your audience members keep notes, select the Blank lines next to slides or Blank lines below slides options in the Write-Up dialog box.

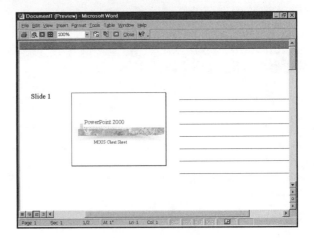

Print a Slide as an Overhead Transparency

An overhead transparency is easy to produce with PowerPoint. You have some choices to make, depending on whether you want color.

To resize the slides in your show for overhead transparencies, click the File menu and select Page Setup. Choose Overhead from the drop-down list under Slides sized for.

Resize for Transpar- encies

You can look at your show in black and white or grayscale by clicking ⬛ Grayscale Preview on the Standard toolbar, or by clicking the View menu and selecting Black and White. In black and white mode, a right-click enables you to see a short-cut menu listing a variety of black, white, and grayscale options (see Objective 38).

If the slide is to be sent to a service bureau or printer, the show can be delivered as a PowerPoint file on disk, or it can be sent via modem. Microsoft included a wizard to send the file to a company called Genigraphics. Files can be sent electronically to Genigraphics, and printed copies will be sent back. To send files electronically, click the File menu and select Send.

TAKE THE TEST

Task 1

This task covers Objectives 38–42.

Some of the tasks in this group cannot be saved in the normal manner. One such task is previewing the show in black and white—that will not be retained when the show is saved. When you take the exam, in some cases you will be asked to set the file up by following directions, and then proceed to the next question. The testing engine will determine whether you have taken the desired actions. For this Practice lab, we will run through the motions and then save a file that can be checked later.

Open the Print Thoughts file from the enclosed CD to begin this task.

1. Preview how the show will appear in black and white.

2. Set up the show to print as an overhead transparency.

3. Format the presentation to print as pure black and white.

4. Set the show to print handouts with two slides on a page.

5. Send the file to Word with blank lines next to the slides.

6. Save the Word document as C:\PP2000\Print.doc. Close Word.

7. Save the PowerPoint show as C:\PP2000\Print Ideas.ppt.

The solution files for this task are Ch09-Print Ideas.ppt and Ch09-Print.doc. To check your work, open Ch06-Great Ideas.ppt. Then open your answer, C:\PP2000\Print Ideas.ppt or C:\PP2000\Print.doc. Click Window on the Menu bar and choose Arrange All. The two shows or documents will be displayed side by side.

Cheat Sheet

Preview Presentation in Black and White

- View, Black and White.

- 🖼 to toggle between color and grayscale.

- 🖼 while holding down the Shift key to see pure Black and White.

- Click the right mouse button on a black and white preview. The Black and White item gives you variations on Black, White, and Gray.

Print Slides in a Variety of Formats

File, Page Setup

File, Print, Print what

Print Audience Handouts

File, Page Setup

File, Print, Print what

Print Speaker Notes in a Specified Format

File, Page Setup

File, Send to

Print a Slide as an Overhead Transparency

File, Page Setup

File, Send to

Delivering a Presentation

This skill set will test your ability to run a PowerPoint slide show. You might be called upon to go forward to a particular slide (press <number>+ENTER) or back up to the previous slide to add more explanation (Page Up). You could use a light pencil or the pointer to call attention to details, but PowerPoint has a built-in pen.

Some of the objectives covered in the test cannot be saved as a file. For example, you cannot save the drawings produced by a pen during the show. The testing engine will be capable of picking this up. When you are asked to perform a task that cannot be saved, pay particular attention to the directions before moving to the next question.

- Start a Slide Show on any Slide
- Use Onscreen Navigation Tools
- Use the Pen During a Presentation

43

Start a Slide Show on Any Slide

By default, clicking the Slide Show icon will start the show from the selected slide. If you want to have more control over which slides are shown, you can set up the show or create a custom show.

Custom Shows

Click the Slide Show menu and select Set Up Show. On the right side of the Set Up Show dialog box is an area that enables you to choose to show All the slides or a range of slides. You can choose the slide to start and end the show.

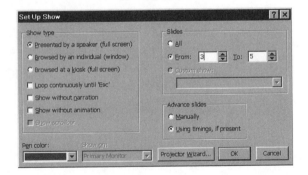

If you want to show the slides in a special order Click the Slide Show menu and select Custom Shows. Click the New button.

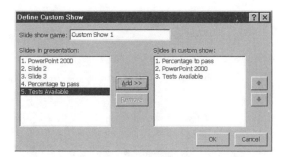

All the slides in the presentation are listed on the left pane in the Define Custom Show dialog box. You can choose which slides to include in the custom show by selecting a slide and clicking Add. To select multiple slides, hold down Ctrl as you select the slides. The arrow keys on the right provide the opportunity to change the presentation order. To move a slide up or down in the presentation order, select the slide and click the up or down arrow. You can also include a slide more than one time without having to include extra copies. After the slides have been selected, enter a name in the Slide show name box and click OK.

Changes made in custom show do not affect the order or numbering of the slides, just their presentation order.

125

44

Use Onscreen Navigation Tools

You can use the keyboard and the mouse to run your slide show.

Shortcuts

When you are in Slide Show view, clicking the right mouse button will display a shortcut menu of navigation, notes, and show options. The test probably will not require you to know all the shortcuts, but knowing a keyboard shortcut option can save precious time during the test. The following table lists some shortcuts for running a slide show.

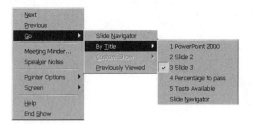

Here are some shortcuts to use while running a slide show. You can press F1 during a slide show to see a list of controls.

Press	To
Enter, Page Down, Right Arrow, Down Arrow, N, or the spacebar (or click the mouse)	Perform the next animation or advance to the next slide

Press	To
Page up, Left arrow, Up arrow, Backspace, or P	Perform the previous animation or return to the previous slide
<number>+Enter	Go to slide <number>
B or period (.)	Display a black screen or return to the slide show from a black screen
W or comma (,)	Display a white screen or return to the slide show from a white screen
S or plus sign (+)	Stop or restart an automatic slide show
Esc, Ctrl+Break,	End a slide show or hyphen (-)
E	Erase onscreen annotations
H	Go to next hidden slide
T	Set new timings while rehearsing
O	Use original timings while rehearsing
M	Use mouse-click to advance while rehearsing
Both mouse buttons for two seconds	Return to the first slide
Ctrl+P	Redisplay hidden pointer or change the pointer to a pen
Ctrl+A	Redisplay hidden pointer or change the pointer to an arrow
Ctrl+H	Hide the pointer and button immediately

continues

Continued

Press	To
Ctrl+U	Hide the pointer and button in 15 seconds
Shift+F10 (or right-click)	Display the shortcut menu
Tab	Go to the first or next hyperlink on a slide
Shift+Tab	Go to the last or previous hyperlink on a slide
Enter	While a hyperlink is selected, perform the "mouse click" behavior of the selected hyperlink
Shift+Enter	While a hyperlink is selected, perform the "mouse over" behavior of the selected hyperlink

Use the Pen During a Presentation

PowerPoint has a feature that enables you to draw on the screen like a television sports commentator during a slide show presentation.

While the show is running press Ctrl+P and the pointer will change to a pen. The other way to bring up the pen is to right-click, choose Pointer Options, and select Pen. The same Pointer Options menu will let you change the color of the pen by selecting Pen Color and clicking the color you want. To write or draw on the slides, hold down the mouse button and move the mouse.

These annotations are temporary. They will disappear when you move to the next slide. To erase the marks on the slide you are viewing, press E on the keyboard.

Annotations

TAKE THE TEST

Task 1

This task covers Objective 43, "Start a Slide Show on Any Slide"; Objective 44, "Use Onscreen Navigation Tools"; and Objective 45, "Use the Pen During a Presentation." To begin this task, open the Show Thoughts file from the CD.

1. Create a Custom show that starts on Slide 2 and runs through Slide 9 (Brainstorming Activity). Name it Short Show.

2. Run the Short Show. Use the Slide Navigator to go to Slide 5.

3. Use the pen to underline What to Expect. Stop the show.

4. Save the PowerPoint show as C;\PP2000\Show Ideas.ppt.

The solution file for this task is Ch10-Show Ideas.ppt. To check your work, open Ch10-Show Ideas.ppt. Then open your answer: C:\PP2000\Show Ideas.ppt. Click Window on the Menu bar and choose Arrange All. The two shows will be displayed side by side. Directions for the task are in Objectives 43–45.

Cheat Sheet

Start a Slide Show on Any Slide

Slide Show, Set Up Show

Slide Show Custom Show

1. Slide Show, Set Up Show.

2. Choose to show all or a range of slides.

Show Slides in a Special Order

1. Slide Show, Custom Shows.

2. Click New.

3. Select a slide and click Add. To select multiple slides, hold down Ctrl as you select.

Use Onscreen Navigation Tools

The right mouse shortcut menu shows navigation, notes, and show options.

Use F1 to see a list of shortcuts.

Use the Pen During a Presentation

Right-click, Pointer Options, Pen (Ctrl+P)

Managing Files

In this series of tasks we'll add a hyperlink and use the Office Assistant. You also will need to master a couple of techniques related to saving the file.

A PowerPoint show can be emailed to others or published on the Web. Follow the test directions closely when you are asked to answer a question related to these two topics.

The test must be capable of capturing your answer regardless of the testing setup. Your email message will not actually be sent and the Web show will be "published" locally. The question will provide the path it wants you to use.

- Insert Hyperlink
- Use the Office Assistant
- Save Changes to a Presentation
- Save As a New Presentation
- Send a Presentation via Email
- Publish a Presentation to the Web

Insert Hyperlink

Hyperlinks are spots on the slide that, when activated, will jump to another slide, file, or location. Hyperlinks can also be set to perform an action. Clicking with the mouse or passing the mouse pointer over the object can activate hyperlinks.

Linking

First select the text or object that you want to use as a hyperlink spot. Click the ▣ Insert Hyperlink (Ctrl+K) icon or right-click and choose Action settings or Hyperlink.

If you choose Hyperlink, PowerPoint asks what the location of the jump is to be.

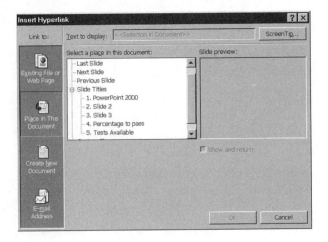

The four links to shortcuts in the Insert Hyperlink dialog box
are as follows:

Existing File or Web Page	Links to an existing document (for example a spreadsheet, database, or Word document) or location on the Internet
Place in this Document	Links to another place within the file
Create New Document	Create a link to a file that you will create later
E-mail Address	Create a link that will create an email message with the selected address on the To line

In the upper-right corner you will find a Screen Tip button. If
you fill in this option, text will appear on the screen when the
pointer passes over the hyperlink.

When the show is run, the pointer will change to a hand as it
passes over a hyperlink. One click is all that's needed to activate
the jump.

Besides the right-mouse button method, you can choose to
Slide Show Action Settings to bring up the Action Settings dia-
log box. Hyperlinks can be set for Mouse Over and Mouse
Click actions.

If you use the Action settings option, you can also create a
Hyperlink to other locations, but the options are limited. You
can link to a URL Web address, but you don't have the ability
to browse offered by the Hyperlink option.

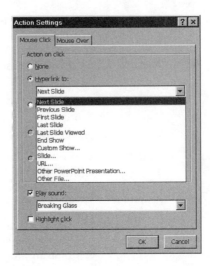

The Action Settings dialog box will enable you to specify a sound to be played when the hyperlink is activated. If the hyperlink is an object, it can be made to appear highlighted.

Active Settings also permit you to set up a *mouse over*—when the pointer passes over the link an action is performed. The Mouse Over actions are performed as if the link had been clicked.

Use the Office Assistant

The Office Assistant is back and out of its cage. Now it has better animation and is not surrounded by a box. The Office Assistant is a cartoon character that will appear to offer advice or give you the opportunity to ask "real" language questions about the program. Eight choices are available on the Office 2000 CD. One of the most popular is Clippit.

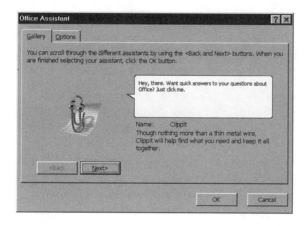

If you don't see Clippit or one of his buddies, click the Help menu and select Show the Office Assistant. You can also bring up the Office Assistant by clicking ? Microsoft PowerPoint Help or using F1.

Show the Assistant

Use the Assistant

If you need help, click on the Assistant, type your question in the Input box, and click Search, or press Enter. To get details, click the relevant sentence to see the Help file topic related to your query.

If you choose Options in the Assistant's balloon, you can select preferences from the Office Assistant dialog box to make the creatures behave the way you want.

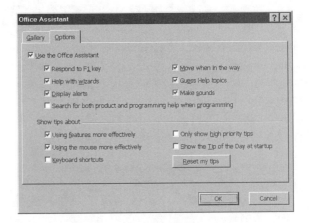

The Options tab determines the Assistant's response, the Gallery tab will let you choose a different character.

Save Changes to a Presentation

Saving regularly is a way to reduce stress in the future. Learn a couple of different ways to save. This is good advice for all the objectives. If an item is grayed out on the menu or a keyboard shortcut is unavailable, you'll need to know alternatives.

Read the instructions carefully. A great majority of the questions will ask you to save before going on to the next question, but some questions could ask you to continue without saving the file.

A presentation can be periodically saved by using any of the following methods:

Quick Save

- Click 🖫 Save on the Standard toolbar.
- Click the File menu and select Save.
- Press Ctrl+S or Shift+F12 on the keyboard.

49

Save As a New Presentation

Save the show under a new name if you would like to use an existing presentation as the skeleton of a new show, or if you want to experiment with a show and not destroy what you already have.

Save As

If you have just started a presentation and have not saved or named it, click 🔲 Save on the Standard toolbar to open the Save As dialog box. You can also save an existing publication under a new name through the Save As dialog.

Click the File menu and select Save As or press (F12) to open the Save As dialog box. First look at the Save In field at the top. Verify that the file will be saved in the location you want. Next give it a name and either press Enter or click Save.

Create a New Folder

You can use 📁 Create New Folder (Alt+5) or highlight the file and use ❌ Delete (Del) to delete existing files from the Save As box. You might not be asked to delete files, but creating a new folder would be a legitimate instruction.

50

Send a Presentation via Email

You can choose to email your show to others. PowerPoint, like the other Office 2000 applications, is capable of being used for workgroup collaboration.

To send a presentation via email, click the File menu and select Send To. Three items pertain to email directly. The first item, Mail Recipient, will send the selected slide as the body of the email message. The next entry Mail Recipient (as Attachment) saves the current show and then opens Outlook with the file as an attachment to an email.

Exchange

The third line, Routing Recipient, walks you through the process of sending a copy of the show to a list of email address; either all at once or routed from one to the other. Click 📧 Mail Recipient on the Standard toolbar to display the same send to options as the ones located on the File menu, except for the routing option.

51

Publish a Presentation to the Web

PowerPoint presentations can make interesting Web site additions. Everyone on your intranet or Internet site can now enjoy the same show that was a hit with your home office. A good reason to put a PowerPoint show on the Web is that you do not need to have PowerPoint installed on your machine to view the presentation.

When a document or show is saved for the Web, a lot of files will be produced. Each picture or background graphic will have its own file. Each slide will have a separate document, and additional files will be produced to make sure that the show will look as good on the Web as it does on your machine.

Save as Web Page

To publish a presentation on the Web, click the File menu and select Save as Web Page. The Save As type box will be set to save the show as a Web Page. Click the Publish button and you will see several options for selecting browser support and what to publish.

The Web Options button on the Publish As a Web Page dialog box exposes more choices for appearance, file formatting, and encoding when saving as a Web page.

On the Web, graphics are not embedded in the documents. When your show is saved as a Web file, a new directory will be created that will hold separate files for graphics, documents, and formatting.

Another way to save a file as a Web document is through the Save As dialog box. Click the File menu and select Save As, or press F12 to open the Save As dialog box. Drop down the Save as Type list at the bottom of the box. Choose Web Page (*.htm;*.html).

Save As

Web pages can be previewed before you save them; click the File menu and select Web Page Preview.

TAKE THE TEST

You've performed some of these tasks before, such as Save changes to a Presentation. One task, Use Office Assistant, cannot be saved as a file.

This task covers Objective 46, "Insert Hyperlink"; Objective 47, "Use the Office Assistant"; Objective 48, "Save Changes to a Presentation"; Objective 49, "Save As a New Presentation"; Objective 50, "Send a Presentation via Email"; and Objective 51, "Publish a Presentation to the Web." To begin this task, open the Final Thoughts file from the CD.

1. Insert a text box near the bottom of Slide 14. Insert the text `Click here for the names of the crew`. Center the text.

2. Make the text a hyperlink to Thank you.doc in the Practice Lab CD.

3. Send the presentation as an attachment to `GeneralSales@mcp.com`.

4. Use the Office Assistant to find troubleshooting hyperlinks. Look at the entry for "When I click a hyperlink, nothing happens."

5. Close the Help file and hide the Office Assistant.

6. Publish the show as `Final Thoughts.htm` to C:\PP2000.

7. Save the file as C:\PP2000\Final Idea.ppt.

The solution file for this task is Ch11-Final Idea.ppt. To check your work, open Ch11-Final Idea.ppt. Then open your answer: C:\PP2000\Final Idea.ppt. Click Window on the menu bar and choose Arrange All. The two shows will be displayed side by side. Directions for the task are in Objectives 46–51.

Save as Web page creates separate files for each slide and each graphic. Other files are created for things like navigation. To look at your Web show, double-click the file C:\PP2000\Final Thoughts.htm. The other components will be in a folder called C:\PP2000\Final Thoughts_files.

Cheat Sheet

Insert Hyperlink

[icon] on the Standard toolbar (Ctrl+K)

Right-click and choose Action settings or Hyperlink

Use the Office Assistant

[icon] on the Standard toolbar (F1)

Save Changes to a Presentation

[icon] File, Save (Ctrl+S)

Shift+F12

Save as a New Presentation

File, Save As (F12)

Send a Presentation via Email

File, Send To

[icon] Mail Recipient on the Standard toolbar

Publish a Presentation to the Web

1. File, Save as Web Page.
2. Click the Publish button.

Preparation Guide

I took my first MOUS exam in September 1997. Since then I have passed all the tests both Proficient and Expert. I have been given the opportunity to participate in forum discussions of the program and to write reviews of the exams. Through that exposure, I've spoken and corresponded with hundreds of people who are taking these tests. What follows are the directions that they have reported as the most valuable.

Test Specs

The exams are hands-on. In other words, there are no multiple choice, Yes/No, or fill in the blank questions. You will be following directions and using the actual application.

Passing is 75–80% correct. You will be given about one hour to complete the test. There is a small leeway given to read the questions—about 20 minutes. As soon as you start to work on the task, the one hour clock starts. The number of questions varies with each exam, but you should expect 40–50.

During the Test

The most important piece of advice concerning the tests is to read the question carefully and don't do any more or less than it asks you. Try to imagine that someone has asked you to do a task and that they will now look at your terminal screen to see the results.

One writer asked why he had failed the exam. He had been working with the product for years and the questions were not difficult to answer. The reason for the failure turned out to be that he had done what the instructions asked, and then saved and closed the document. Unless you are specifically asked to do so, leave the answer exposed on the screen when you move to the next question.

Don't change the view unless you are asked to do so. Do not obscure the view of the answer by leaving dialog boxes or toolbars floating over the slide.

Follow all the instructions that are given to you at the test site. If you have any problems with your machine at the testing center, bring it to the attention of the administrator immediately.

Be Prepared

You will have a limited amount of time to complete the test. Do not count on using the Help file to find information. Try to learn more than one way to do a job—there is usually a keyboard equivalent for items on the menu bar. You will be scored on your results. In the past, some options have been grayed out, forcing the user to find alternative means.

The Office 2000 Cheat Sheet has been designed to help you learn alternative methods of accomplishing tasks. After each practice element, the Cheat Sheet short list details in abbreviated form any steps or terms that are used in the chapter. The Cheat Sheet short list can also be used by the reader as a quick reference during the practice session.

The tearcard inside the front cover of this book also includes tables that outline the various methods for issuing a command: keyboard shortcuts, toolbar buttons, and Menu command strings. Tear out the card and use it to review the shortcuts in the last few minutes before stepping into the exam room.

You will not be allowed to bring any books or papers into the testing area, so use the tearcard and Cheat Sheets for review, but do not become dependent on them.

For More Information

The main Web site for information about the exams is http://www.MOUS.NET. This site will also give you directions to an Authorized Testing Center (ACT). Call 1-800-933-4493 if you need more details.

The program is international. If you live in Japan, Brazil, or Latin America, there is information concerning test sites and local variations.

There are some news groups that have formed to discuss the tests. Try msnews.microsoft.com, and go to either microsoft.public.cert.exam.mous or microsoft.public. certification.office.

There is also an online "magazine" at `http://OfficeCert.com`. `OfficeCert.com` has a discussion forum and articles relating to the examinations, the applications, and job hunting techniques.

Take a Break

The standard advice you receive for every potentially stressful situation also applies to the MOUS exam.

Get a good night's sleep before the test. If you don't know it by then, it's probably too late to try to pound it into your head. The tearcard and Cheat Sheets will give you an opportunity to review the skills that you will use, but they are not a substitute for good practice sessions.

Think of the whole experience as a fun adventure. Enjoy your experience. When the test is over, the administrator will give you a copy of your score. If you miss the breaking point for passing, the printout will suggest areas of study.

After the test, you can review your score and weak areas. The Cheat Sheet books are developed using the Objectives and Activities that make up the examination. The Appendix of each book includes the objective list and the location in the book where you can find a discussion of that task.

When you see that you have passed, quietly shout Hurrah! (quietly because others might still be taking the test). Keep your printout and wait about four to six weeks for your certificate.

Good luck to you. You can do it.

Objectives Index

Standardized Coding Number	Activity	Chapter Number	Objective Number	Page Number
	PP2000.1 Creating a Presentation			
PP2000.1.1	Delete slides	2	8	
PP2000.1.2	Create a specified type of slide	2	7	
PP2000.1.3	Create a presentation from a template or a wizard	1	3	
PP2000.1.4	Navigate among different views (Slide, Outline, Sorter, Tri-pane)	1	1	
PP2000.1.5	Create a new presentation from existing slides	1	4	
PP2000.1.6	Copy a slide from one presentation into another	2	6	

continues

Continued

Standardized Coding Number	Activity	Chapter Number	Objective Number	Page Number
PP2000.1 Creating a Presentation				
PP2000.1.7	Insert headers and footers	3	13	
PP2000.1.8	Create a blank presentation	1	5	
PP2000.1.9	Create a presentation using the AutoContent Wizard	1	2	
PP2000.1.10	Send a presentation via email	11	50	
PP2000.2 Modifying a Presentation				
PP2000.2.1	Change the order of slides using Slide Sorter view	3	10	
PP2000.2.2	Find and replace text	4	16	
PP2000.2.3	Change the layout for one or more slides	3	14	
PP2000.2.4	Change slide layout (Modify the Slide Master)	3	12	
PP2000.2.5	Modify slide sequence in the outline pane	3	11	

Standardized Coding Number	Activity	Chapter Number	Objective Number	Page Number
	PP2000.2 Modifying a Presentation			
PP2000.2.6	Apply a design template	2	9	
	PP2000.3 Working with Text			
PP2000.3.1	Check spelling	4	15	
PP2000.3.2	Change and replace text fonts (individual slide and entire presentation)	4	17	
PP2000.3.3	Enter text in Tri-pane view	4	20	
PP2000.3.4	Import text from Word	5	25	
PP2000.3.5	Change the text alignment	4	18	
PP2000.3.6	Create a text box for entering text	5	22	
PP2000.3.7	Use the Wrap text in AutoShape feature	5	23	
PP2000.3.8	Use the Office Clipboard	5	24	
PP2000.3.9	Use the Format Painter	4	19	

continues

Continued

Standardized Coding Number	Activity	Chapter Number	Objective Number	Page Number
	PP2000.2 Modifying a Presentation			
PP2000.3.10	Promote and Demote text in slide and outline panes	4	21	
	PP2000.4 Working with Visual Elements			
PP2000.4.1	Add a picture from the ClipGallery	6	26	
PP2000.4.2	Add and group shapes using WordArt or the Drawing toolbar	6	27	
PP2000.4.3	Apply formatting	7	31	
PP2000.4.4	Place text inside a shape using a text box	7	30	
PP2000.4.5	Scale and size an object including ClipArt	7	29	
PP2000.4.6	Create tables within PowerPoint	7	32	
PP2000.4.7	Rotate and fill an object	6	28	

Standardized Coding Number	Activity	Chapter Number	Objective Number	Page Number
PP2000.5 Customizing a Presentation				
PP2000.5.1	Add AutoNumber bullets	8	33	
PP2000.5.2	Add speaker notes	8	37	
PP2000.5.3	Add graphical bullets	8	34	
PP2000.5.4	Add slide transitions	8	35	
PP2000.5.5	Animate text and objects	8	36	
PP2000.6 Creating Output				
PP2000.6.1	Preview presentation in black and white	9	38	
PP2000.6.2	Print slides in a variety of formats	9	39	
PP2000.6.3	Print audience handouts	9	40	
PP2000.6.4	Print speaker notes in a specified format	9	41	

continues

Continued

Standardized Coding Number	Activity	Chapter Number	Objective Number	Page Number
PP2000.7 Delivering a Presentation				
PP2000.7.1	Start a slide show on any slide	10	43	
PP2000.7.2	Use onscreen navigation tools	10	44	
PP2000.7.3	Print a slide as an overhead transparency	9	42	
PP2000.7.4	Use the pen during a presentation	10	45	
PP2000.8 Managing Files				
PP2000.8.1	Save changes to a presentation	11	48	
PP2000.8.2	Save as a new presentation	11	49	
PP2000.8.3	Publish a presentation to the Web	11	51	
PP2000.8.4	Use Office Assistant	11	47	
PP2000.8.5	Insert hyperlink	11	46	

Index

CD-ROM Installation

Windows 95/NT Installation Instructions

1. Insert the CD-ROM disc into your CD-ROM drive.

2. From the Windows 95/NT desktop, double-click the My Computer icon.

3. Double-click the icon representing your CD-ROM drive.

4. Double-click the icon titled START.EXE to run the CD-ROM interface.

If Windows 95/NT is installed on your computer and you have the AutoPlay feature enabled, the START.EXE program starts automatically whenever you insert the disc into your CD-ROM drive.